THE NATIONAL TRUST BOOK OF GREAT HOUSES OF BRITAIN

THE
NATIONAL
TRUST
BOOK OF

GREAT HOUSES OF BRITAIN

Nigel Nicolson

Book Club Associates
London

This edition published 1978 by
Book Club Associates
by arrangement with Weidenfeld and Nicolson
and The National Trust

Designed by Raymond Carpenter

Colour separations by Newsele Litho Ltd, Milan

Printed in Great Britain by
Cox & Wyman Ltd
London, Fakenham and Reading

The endpapers show Easton Neston

CONTENTS

(NT): National Trust

(NTS): National Trust for Scotland

Foreword

IN ITS ORIGINAL EDITION, this book was published by Weidenfeld & Nicolson in 1965, and then by the Hamlyn Publishing Group in 1968. For some years it has been out of print. Now that the original publishers and the National Trust have agreed to publish books of common interest under their joint imprint, the book is reissued in a different format and with much new material, both textual and photographic.

Eight houses which were described and illustrated in the first edition have been omitted, and eight others replace them. The 'new' houses are Felbrigg, Erddig, Saltram, Ditchley and Plas Newydd, and three which were described in my other book *Great Houses of the Western World* (Weidenfeld & Nicolson, 1968), namely Penshurst, Castle Fraser and Petworth. Many of the original photographs by Kerry Dundas have been retained to illustrate the 'old' houses, but in some cases they have been supplemented or replaced by more recent photographs commissioned by the National Trust. The new houses, of which five are properties of the Trust, have either been photographed specially for this edition, or are illustrated by photographs which the Trust already possessed. The detailed credits will be found on the last page.

In reconstructing the book, I have tried to vary as widely as possible the dates, size, style and location of the thirty-nine selected houses, in order to form a panorama of British domestic architecture from the early Middle Ages until the last century. I have rewritten many descriptions of the 'old' houses to take account of changes made to them since 1965, and I have revisited most of them for this edition. In describing the additional houses I have given more attention than previously to their present condition, thinking it important to illustrate the different methods employed to save a great house from falling apart (like Erddig), to make it habitable by its family (like Plas Newydd) when economic conditions have greatly changed, to adapt it (like Ditchley) for a use remote from the intentions of its original builders, and to display it to the public (like Saltram and, again, Erddig).

All the houses described are at present opened regularly or periodically to the public, with the exception of Easton Neston and Mereworth Castle.

NIGEL NICOLSON   *Sissinghurst Castle, Kent*

St Michael's
Mount
Cornwall

FEW NOTABLE HOUSES IN BRITAIN lie within sight of the sea. It provided too spectacular and competitive a background for the taste of the sixteenth to eighteenth centuries, when proprietors preferred to look landwards over their farms and parks, the source and symbol of their wealth. The sea was hostile, public and cold. In their eyes St Michael's Mount would have combined every possible disadvantage as a gentleman's seat. It was difficult of access, swept by gales, exposed to piratical attack and the gaze of the curious, and absurdly unsuited to the architecture and landscape-gardening of the times. Besides, the place was not a house at all. It was a fortified monastery, grim and melancholy in its associations and aspect.

In the nineteenth century the reputation of the Mount changed completely, and today we are the inheritors of the romantic tradition that no place in England is more dramatic in its situation nor more subtle in the composition of its different parts. St Michael's Mount is an island – and yet not quite an island, for twice in every twenty-four hours the tide sweeps back from its northern side to expose a causeway, a quarter of a mile long, over which you can walk dryshod to Marazion on the mainland shore. At high spring-tide eighteen feet of water cover the causeway, and this diurnal ebb and flow, controlled as it seems by distant sluice-gates, governs the life of the St Aubyn family who have lived here for over three hundred years.

At the full tide no island appears more perfectly insular, cupped in the inner curve of Mount's Bay like a Hebridean fortress. Its form is that of a nearly symmetrical cone, a mile in circumference at its base and rising in rocky and partly wooded slopes to a peak three hundred feet high. On the summit stands the church with the house below it, extending by their granite walls and towers the upward sweep of the rock so that from a distance it is almost impossible to tell where the rock ends and the building begins. From Marazion the house has the appearance of a coronet of stone, less a structure than a sudden tightening of the natural rock.

Once ashore, an entirely new aspect of the Mount is revealed. It is now seen to be semi-tropical in its flowers and vegetation. The sturdy little harbour, with the white boatmen's cottages, is everybody's dream picture of a Cornish fishing village. As one climbs the steep cobbled pathway to the summit,

*An air-view of the Mount looking
north-east at high tide, when the rock is
completely cut off from the mainland.
The circuit of harbour and Mount is
almost exactly one mile.*

To Sr. John St. Aubyn, of Clowance in the COUNTY of CORNWALL Bar. One of the Representatives of the said County. THIS NORTH EAST VIEW OF St. MICHAEL'S MOUNT. Is most humbly Inscribed by his most Obed. Hum.ble Servant Richard Scaddan

St Michael's Mount looking west towards
Penzance, from a drawing by Richard Scaddan
in the mid-eighteenth century. The height and
cragginess of the Mount is considerably
exaggerated.

following the pilgrims' route to St Michael's shrine, one is back again in the Middle Ages. Each difficult step upwards is both a penance and a pleasure. The view widens over the great sweep of the bay. Overhead, a Cornish cross on a jutting rock, the ruins of a watch-tower, a battery of guns, the solid soaring walls of close-set masonry, make one wonder what this place can be – a church, a castle, a relic or a private house? The Mount is all these things. Apart from its incomparable situation, its chief fascination lies in the mingling of truth with fantasy, as its history emerges from legend into recorded fact.

St Michael's Mount has been known by that name *Mons Sancti Michaelis de Cornubia*, since at least the time of Edward the Confessor. By lifting one of the pew-seats in the choir of the church, one can expose a tight spiral staircase leading downwards to a vaulted cell cut in the rock. Only guesswork can supply an explanation of it. It could be a hermit's cell dating from the darkest ages of English history, a priest's hole, or a dungeon, or even a tomb, for a skeleton was found in it when the cell was discovered in 1720. But there is no doubt about the significance of the lovely cruciform church above it. In 1070 St Michael's Mount was granted by Robert, Count of Mortain, to Mont Saint Michel in Normandy, the great abbey which resembles the Cornish Mount not only in name but in situation, for it too is built on the summit of a rock which becomes an island at high tide. St Michael's Mount was one of its dependent priories, and a church was built there in 1135 by Bernard, Abbot of Mont Saint Michel. It had a Prior and twelve monks, selected from the brothers of the French abbey, to which it owed obedience and sixteen marks a year. For nearly three hundred and fifty years, until 1414, the Cornish Mount remained attached to the Norman Mount, the strength of the ties between them varying with the current state of tension between England and France. In wartime the priory was taken into the hands of the English king; with the return of peace, it was honourably restored to the French. Without intermission, it was a place of pilgrimage, for it contained important relics, and from the revenues of the farms, harbour, annual fair, and the offerings of the pilgrims, it prospered greatly.

The existing church is not Abbot Bernard's original, which was destroyed by an earthquake in 1275. A new church was raised on the foundations of the old late in the fourteenth century, and the present windows were added about fifty years later, together with the Lady Chapel, a lovely casket of carved stone which stands on the highest point of the Mount beside the church. By this time St Michael's Mount had passed by the gift of Henry VI from the French abbey into the hands of the Bridgettine convent of Syon, Middlesex. The Abbess of Syon held it for over a hundred years until the dissolution of both foundations in 1539. This disaster did not affect the Mount as much as its mother convent, since the number of monks had declined to as few as two or three, and for many years its importance as a fortress had overshadowed its religious significance. Occupying a strategic and almost impregnable position near the south-west tip of England, it became a gateway for revolution and a bastion of defence. It was seized by the King's enemies in 1194, recaptured, fortified, garrisoned, attacked by pirates, corsairs, pretenders and English rebels, a

bone of contention in the Hundred Years' War, the Wars of the Roses and the Civil War. One must picture the Mount throughout these centuries as fulfilling a double role, the priory sheltering behind the garrison, the Prior and Governor, monks and soldiers, sharing the cramped quarters folded round the upper part of the rock. It was here that the Earl of Oxford landed from France in 1471 with a posse of men disguised as pilgrims; here that Perkin Warbeck raised the standard of his ill-fated revolt; from here that Humphrey Arundell launched the Cornish rebellion of 1549; and from here that the Spanish Armada was first sighted, according to Macaulay,

> *For swift to east and swift to west the ghastly war-flame spread.*
> *High on St Michael's Mount it shone; it shone on Beachy Head.*

Chevy Chase, the former refectory of the Monks. It takes its name from the seventeenth-century plaster frieze depicting a hunt in full cry. The royal coat-of-arms at the far end is that of Charles I, and is dated 1641.

Queen Elizabeth sold the Mount to Robert Cecil, first Earl of Salisbury, in 1599, and from the Cecils it passed to Francis Basset, who held it for the King in 1646. It came to the Cornish family of St Aubyn in 1657, and the garrison was soon afterwards disbanded. For many years the Mount remained virtually unoccupied. But during the eighteenth century the St Aubyns began to use it as an occasional summer home, and converted the Lady Chapel into the charming drawing-rooms that one sees today. But it was too small a house, too inconvenient in its site and monastic-military layout, for use as a permanent residence by a landed family. It was not until 1875 that the old rock was scoured and blasted to provide the foundations for a great new block of rooms which make the Mount, in spite of its exposure to the Atlantic winds, one of the most comfortable houses in the country.

This latest phase in the history of St Michael's Mount is usually dismissed as a misfortune or unworthy of serious attention. In fact its Victorian additions are among the greatest achievements of nineteenth-century domestic architecture. The architect was Piers St Aubyn, a cousin of the owner, who is otherwise known for his restorations of Cornish churches and the Temple Church in London. His problem was both aesthetic and structural. The top of the Mount was hallowed ground, not only for its religious and historical associations, but for the world-famous silhouette which it presented from the mainland shore. It could not be radically disturbed. But below the parapet level there was nothing but precipitous rock. St Aubyn solved the problem by erecting his new building in the form of a tall, wide tower set against the south-eastern face, invisible from the mainland. Its foot rests upon the bedrock half-way down the slope, its summit rises almost, but not quite, to the level of the original buildings, which are thus left untrammelled by modern additions and continue to crown the Mount as they had for the previous seven hundred years. The workmanship is everywhere superb. The whole is built of silver-coloured granite which outcrops into the body of the house as staircases, cornices and window-frames, so that the visitor feels himself suspended in a huge cage of stone. Outside the double-windows is the cry of gulls and the continuous rumble of the sea.

Most great houses are fusions of different styles of architecture. St Michael's Mount is a fusion of functions dictated by the extraordinary nature of the site. Because it is all built of the same granite, and because its shiplike exposure necessitated at every period the same massiveness of construction, every part of it from the twelfth century to the nineteenth blends into a whole. From the terraces contrived on the knobbly summit of a Gibraltar one looks across and downwards at a scurry of small boats or at a procession of approaching visitors. It is not difficult to translate this view into the mediaeval terms of carracks and pilgrims. If a rock is a symbol of permanence, a house on a rock is a symbol of continuity. This is the dominant impression left by St Michael's Mount. It is gay on a summer's day, and majestic in a storm. It can never have been very different.

A drawing of the south-eastern additions designed by Piers St Aubyn in 1873–8, when the old priory-fortress was transformed into a comfortable private house.

Ightham Mote
Kent

ONE OF THE HAPPIEST OF THE MANY LEGENDS about Ightham Mote is that Cromwell's soldiers, intent on destroying it as a Royalist stronghold, got lost in the deep wooded valleys of the Weald and ransacked another house of lesser interest instead. Thus Ightham passed safely through another crisis in its remarkably long life. It was saved on this occasion by its seclusion. Between two main roads from London to the Kentish coast a network of lanes increases more than clarifies the intricacies of this rich countryside of arable and fruit. So deep have the old drover's tracks been worn by centuries of traffic that they have become less like roads than tunnels through the woods. At the foot of one of them the screen parts for an instant to reveal a house wholly in keeping with the privacy of its approach. It is deliberately hidden, hugging the ground like an animal its den.

Ightham is built round four sides of a courtyard and is surrounded by a moat. The moat is so much part of it – indeed almost the essence of it – that the casual visitor could be forgiven for imagining that the 'Mote' of its name is an earlier spelling of the word. It is nothing of the sort. It recalls the *moot* or local council which in the Middle Ages met in the most prosperous house of each neighbourhood, and the name alone would be a sufficient indication of its antiquity. But the buildings themselves proclaim it. They form the ideal image of an early English manor-house, one of the few genuine examples of a style which dominated English building for three hundred years.

We can safely begin in the early fourteenth century. The manor then belonged to a Sir Thomas Cawne, and it was he who erected the buildings on the east or inner side of the courtyard. They comprised a Great Hall, a chapel, a crypt below it (which is possibly a survival from a yet earlier house), a kitchen, a solar and one or two bedrooms. In its essentials the whole of this house survives. It was extremely uncomfortable. The stone and timber roof of the hall, although a splendid piece of engineering, was designed to collect the smoke from the central hearth and release it through gaps in the upper beams, but its great height made the fire almost ineffective as a means of warming the hall. There was no dais to separate the master's table from the servants', no oriel window to grace its walls, no decorated screen at the servants' end, no musicians' gallery. The hall was the centre of the household's life, rush-strewn

The main entrance, with its original fifteenth-century doors. To the left and right are the parapets of the stone bridge which crosses the moat.

and squalid, and its magnificence can be enjoyed better today than at any period when it was serving its original purpose. At a later date, during the fifteenth century, a fireplace and chimney were substituted for the open hearth, and a broad window of five tall lights was inserted in the west wall overlooking the courtyard. The old chapel and the crypt are even more massively austere, rooms that you might find in a Sicilian monastery, almost Norman in the grouping of their rounded stone, and even the kitchen has the same character of quasi-ecclesiastical architecture. One room only begins to foreshadow later standards of gentility. The solar on the upper floor, ancestor of the Saloon and modern drawing-room, ensured at least some privacy for the women of the house.

This was the house that served the Cawnes and their successors, the De Hauts, for about a hundred and forty years, say from 1340 to 1480. Then two other sides of the quadrangle were built, the west and the south. On the west or entrance side a central tower of three storeys was erected at the inner end of the bridge, and it was flanked by a large room on each side with bedrooms and another drawing-room above. A similar wing, possibly built on the lower courses of an earlier building, was added on the south side. At the same time improvements were made to the original house. One can visualize from the existing buildings the De Hauts' tussle with mediaeval inconvenience and their resistance to the temptation to pull the whole thing down and start afresh.

The last major addition was the work of Sir Richard Clement in about 1520. He closed the north side of the quadrangle by a new chapel in the form of a timber framework overhanging the moat, with an open cloister beneath it. This chapel, together with the hall, is the chief glory of Ightham. In inspiration it is still Gothic. Its barrel-vaulted roof, richly ornamented with the Tudor rose and portcullis, its six windows inset with Dutch sixteenth-century stained glass, its pews, the tracery of its lovely screen, its hooded pulpit and linenfold panelling round the walls, all illustrate superbly the transitional

style which the Continental Renaissance had begun to influence. In this way the courtyard was squared off as we see it today, and externally the house dropped its walls clean into the water of the moat on all four sides.

It had taken three centuries, the fourteenth, fifteenth and sixteenth, to create this delightful compactness. There was no more space to build, and when the Elizabethan owners, the Allens, needed more room for staff and stables, they were obliged to build a second quadrangle outside. Part of this survives. In any other place, these buildings would themselves be worthy of a pilgrimage, but at Ightham they can pass almost unnoticed. It is the water around the main house that first catches and holds your attention: the moat, the pool below it, the waterfall above it. And then the texture of the buildings: cobbles underfoot, walls of weathered native materials, patched unself-consciously and each bearing some mark of its originator – a moulding, a chamfering, a pattern of leaded diamond panes, a carved head grimacing under the weight of a beam or peering cockney-like from the corner of a door.

But inevitably, and not to its disadvantage, the house bears evidence that it has been in almost continuous occupation since it was completed. There are Jacobean fireplaces, friezes and staircases; a Venetian window of the late seventeenth century and hand-painted wallpaper of the same period; windows of Walpole Gothic in the courtyard; some pretty Victorian bedrooms and an imitation of Tudor linenfold in the corridors. All these are due to the Selby family who owned the Mote between 1598 and 1889 – three centuries reduced to a mere incident in its history. In the early twentieth century the Colyer-Fergussons added some heavy oak embellishments to its interior. They obliterated nothing of significance, and they saved the house from falling to pieces.

Apart from the De Hauts and the Selbys, no family has long been in occupation of the Mote. It seemed destined to a constant change of owner, which explains the absence of any written records of its history and of any furniture dating back to its earlier periods. But the latest phase in the story is not the least remarkable. Ightham Mote belongs today to an American, C. H. Robinson. He first fell in love with the Mote when he saw a picture of it in an art-dealer's shop in London, and a few years later, on a bicycling-tour of England, he visited it. The idea began to take root in his mind that one day, perhaps, he might make it his own. The chance came thirty years later, in 1953. The Colyer-Fergussons could no longer afford to maintain a house that can quickly drain a fortune, and put it up for sale. They did not know of Mr Robinson's secret wish, nor he of their intention. The house found no buyer able to live in it, and it was again in danger of demolition. At the last moment Mr Robinson discovered the threat, and the house discovered Mr Robinson. He bought it. He repaired it. He refurnished it. He remade its lovely eighteenth-century garden. For several months in the year, as his commitments in the United States allow, he lives there. It is now his intention to make arrangements that the house shall survive his death, for he believes rightly that such a place, hidden though it is from its nearest neighbours in the Weald, has an enduring significance for the whole English-speaking world and should not be allowed to perish.

Haddon Hall
Derbyshire

IN THIS PART OF DERBYSHIRE scarcely a rock breaks the smoothness of the countryside, which swings, like the roads, in easy rounded gradients. The setting of Haddon is not therefore precipitous, although nineteenth-century water-colourists did their best to make it appear so. The house lies on a spur of a gentle hill above the River Wye which loops round its foot like a casually dropped ribbon. But the approach to the main gate certainly does give a first impression of strength and fortification. The path slopes steeply upwards for the last fifty yards towards a battlemented tower, and to the left of it are climbing turrets and knobbly projections that might have formed the sole inspiration of the romantic revival. This pageantry is not contrived. Not one of these buildings is less than four hundred years old, and the oldest dates back to the thirteenth century. They have grown together from necessity or convenience. The authenticity of Haddon is what makes it so endearing. Its simplicity, its sheer age, its fusion of styles, periods and needs, give it unity. The same grey gritstone, limestone and home-grown oak are used in every part of its construction. There is not a brick, not an ornamental piece of marble, in the whole building.

Haddon has worn well. It was solidly built, and although the Dukes of Rutland did not inhabit it during the eighteenth and nineteenth centuries, they kept its roof and main timbers in repair. Where its materials are roughened by time or use, they are still serviceable because they were originally as sound as simple craftsmanship could make them. A huge block of stone on the threshold of a gate or doorway may be worn into a deep groove by the tread of innumerable feet guided into exactly the same place century after century, but there is no need to replace it. A thick baulk of elm forming a table-top is scarred by knife-cuts, stained with wine and pitted by beetle-holes; after three hundred years you turn it over, and it is good for another three hundred. The entrance courtyard was so well paved that for all its unevenness and irregularity it can look little different today than it did in the thirteenth century. But perhaps the timelessness of Haddon is best sensed in the old kitchen, where can be seen the root of a huge oak which served generations of scullions as a chopping-block, and great vats and troughs which bear traces of the pounding, stirring and scouring to which they were

daily subjected. Even the grand apartments are formed by the same combination of sturdiness and makeshift. Haddon can never have been a luxurious place, although it was the scene of much revelry and display; and even its Elizabethan owners never advanced much beyond carved panels and doorways, journeymen's paintings on the chapel walls and modest family crests in the dining-room. The mediaeval hall suited the Vernons and Manners of the Renaissance, and while they might add a parlour here, a gallery there, the house retained its old ground-plan and character. Without conscious antiquarianism, their restraint was a tribute to the building of their predecessors.

Thus, although Haddon achieved its greatest splendour in the last years of the sixteenth century, it is still the finest example of an English manor-house surviving from the Middle Ages. A house, let it be stressed, not a castle – a house struggling out of the chrysalis of mediaevalism. The original licence to surround it by a wall in the 1190s specified that the wall was not to be more than twelve feet high and was not to be crenellated (*muro exaltato xij pedibus sine kernello*, reads the document preserved at Belvoir), and throughout its history Haddon was never to withstand a siege. Most of its surviving walls and many of its rooms date from the fourteenth century, and one can be certain that the mediaeval extent of the house was not very different from that which we see today.

It was formed around two courtyards, an upper and a lower, each approached by a separate archway, the first for wheeled vehicles, the second for visitors on foot or horseback. The Vernons seem to have strained to the limit the ban on fortification. Although there was originally no crenellation, there were certainly watch-towers rising above the roof-line, and the builders were careful to see that the outer walls were stout and not weakened by too many external windows. But within the courtyards one finds evidence that comfort and feudal dignity were beginning to assume as much importance as defence.

The hall with its attendant kitchens and buttery divides one court from the other. It is approached by a wide flight of steps which lead to an arched opening. Immediately inside is a passage behind the screens, through which one glimpses a large, but not immodestly large, banqueting hall, with a dais for the family's table at the far end, a fireplace on one side and windows on both. This was the normal mediaeval arrangement of the heart of a house, which in essentials was to last until the beginning of the seventeenth century. At Haddon other rooms straggle round the two courts, neater individually than their haphazard arrangement would suggest, and they illustrate that the design of great manor-houses was already being influenced by the need for rooms of several purposes. The whole complex culminates in the Long Gallery, now known as the ball-room, a beautiful room one hundred and ten feet long, panelled throughout in oak and carved walnut. It is almost the only room in the house which reflects the full spirit of the Renaissance. It was built over the existing walls by John Manners and his wife, Dorothy Vernon, daughter and heiress of Sir George Vernon, in the last years of the sixteenth

The lower courtyard from just inside the main entrance. In the centre is the archway leading to the Great Hall. The whole of this range dates from the fourteenth century, apart from the Tudor windows.

OPPOSITE ABOVE *The south front, from one of the terraces. The upper windows are those of the Long Gallery, and at the far end is the fourteenth-century chapel.*

OPPOSITE BELOW *The Long Gallery or ball-room, reconstructed by Sir John Manners before his death in 1611. It is 110 feet long, panelled in oak and embellished by carved walnut, one of the latest and loveliest of long galleries in Britain.*

RIGHT *Medallions which probably represent Henry VII and his wife Elizabeth of York carved in the panelling of the dining-room.*

23

century. Their marriage, following an elopement to which legend has attached details that belong more properly to romantic fiction, took Haddon to the Manners, later Earls and Dukes of Rutland, from whose hands the property has never since passed.

Early in the present century the ninth Duke of Rutland restored the house as nearly as possible to its condition when his ancestors left Haddon for Belvoir in 1701. As quite a young boy he had determined to make this his life's major interest, and set himself to study the architecture of its many periods, so that in converting Haddon into a summer home for his family he would not be guilty of solecisms. Even before his succession to the Dukedom, he embarked on his immense task. Haddon was not a ruin, but its roof was in danger of collapse, the stonework of the windows was perishing, it was almost empty of furniture and its lighting, heating, sanitary and cooking arrangements were as they had been two hundred years before. The only running water in the house, for instance, entered the old kitchen by one conduit and left it by another. The work was sufficiently advanced by 1927 for the Duke to move in, but the restoration continued for several years afterwards. Let not the reader be dismayed by the word 'restoration'. Nothing was faked. The Duke merely replaced what had decayed by materials cut or quarried on the estates from which the original materials had come. Where the restoration required new work so extensive that it involved an almost complete rebuilding, as, for instance, in the roofing of the hall, new timbers were cut at Haddon or Belvoir and erected in such a manner that nobody could possibly mistake the new work for the old.

This latest phase in the history of Haddon is by no means its least glorious. The devotion of this nobleman, the present Duke's father, saved for the nation a house of much more than antiquarian interest. Haddon is the loveliest of the transitional houses of the Middle Ages. The terraced gardens, descending by flower-strewn grey walls to the river beneath, support a rambling building that immediately entrances every visitor. The first impression is not a fleeting one. The charm of Haddon increases with knowledge of its history and exploration of its hidden corners. Its theatrical appearance is due simply to its length of life. We must beware of tingeing our admiration with sentimentality, for its builders would not have known the meaning of the word.

Penshurst Place
Kent

IT IS ONLY POSSIBLE TO DESCRIBE this beautiful, puzzling house historically. For not only do the names of its many owners read like the dramatis personae of all Shakespeare's historical plays combined, but it grew slowly for three centuries, and then for three more was repaired, modernized, re-Gothicized and in part rebuilt. No owner was indifferent to what he found; each added to it or adapted it. In consequence there are few places in Britain more teasing to the archaeologist who attempts to date its various parts, and few where the ordinary visitor will find so much to illustrate how men built and lived (and therefore how they thought) throughout those six centuries.

The house is loosely knit. Almost every part of it is but one room thick. Wing was added to wing at different times, and brick was piled on earlier stone. Mediaeval towers were left isolated or incorporated in a Tudor structure. You need a ground-plan to find your way about the rooms and centuries. But Penshurst is only romantic to those who sentimentalize ancient disarray. It is tough and vigorous. Apart from the Long Gallery, there are no interiors which set out to charm. Yet it is a very seductive house. Because it is so spread-out, shaped roughly like the arms of a swastika, it is full of light. One wing closes the view from another, forming three-sided courtyards and skylines of chimneys, dormers, gables, towers and battlements. It looks outwards too. There is a park and a lovely walled garden, each, like the house, the product of slow maturity. Penshurst is still as Ben Johnson described it after a visit there in 1616, in one of the most elaborate thank-you letters ever penned to a host and hostess:

> *Thou art not, Penshurst, built to envious show,*
> *Of touch, or marble; nor can boast a row*
> *Of polished pillars, or a roofe of gold:*
> *Thou hast no lantherne, whereof tales are told;*
> *Or staire, or courts; but stand'st an ancient pile,*
> *And these grudg'd at, art reverenc'd the while . . .*
> *Now, Penshurst, they that will proportion thee*
> *With other edifices, when they see*
> *Those proud, ambitious heaps, and nothing else,*
> *May say, their lords have built, but thy lord dwells.*

One can confidently begin the story in 1340, not with documents or enigmatic foundations, but with a building still so complete, so striking, that in any other place everything that came after it would seem an anti-climax. The original fourteenth-century manor – or all of it that matters – stands at the centre of the present house. It consisted of porch, hall, undercroft, solar and servants' quarters. Perhaps there was also a chapel and an entrance gateway with an encircling wall, for it is unlikely that the porch led directly out of fields, but if so, these have gone, like the kitchen which lay outside the main hall-block, connected to it by a central passage. You still enter the house by the hall. There has been no other entrance to it from the court since the late eighteenth century, when the side-door was walled up. It makes a staggering first impression. It is very large, its roof spanning nearly forty feet at a single leap without internal columns, and it has remained unaltered since it was built soon after 1340 by Sir John Pulteney, a Mayor of London who purchased the manor in that year.

The hall could almost date from a century earlier, so little change had there been since wealthy men first began to build their halls at ground level instead of on the first floor of a keep. There is a low dais at one end – a six-inch step to separate master from servants – a gallery supported by a screen at the other, two fair-sized rooms beyond it above the larder and buttery, huge windows in each side-wall and high up in the gables, a timber roof, and a brick-tiled floor. It is indescribably empty. There was no fireplace, and none was added later. Instead, an octagonal hearth was laid with logs in the middle of the floor, and the smoke billowed up, free and blinding, to escape from the roof by a louvre. Several long tables, of which two, dating from about 1450, survive, were arranged lengthwise down the centre. It is a barn glorified, a nave secularized. The daily assembly of the entire household in the hall was as traditional as the congregation of the whole village in the parish church, and the only known method of enclosing rooms large enough for both purposes was by building high: the greater the space to be spanned, the higher the roof to span it, like a ship's hull in reverse.

The result is a superb piece of architecture. Its obvious inconvenience makes it all the more remarkable that it has remained untouched for so long. One can only guess at the motives of later owners of Penshurst for saving it, for its survival is almost unique, and only in the last two hundred years have antiquarian interests prevailed over ridicule of such uncouth splendour. The hall, however, had its advantages. It could be used for great occasions in the summer; smaller, more serviceable, rooms were incorporated in its structure at either end; and no doubt the storage space was found useful. So solidly was it built, that the main hall required no major repairs until 1910, and it would have been almost as expensive to demolish it as to build it anew. One reads of a payment in 1471 to a man for catching hawks in the upper rafters, but there is no mention of structural defects. So it was allowed to stand intact. It formed a great central mass to which buildings could be added. It became a hub and perhaps a symbol: very gradually it became an object of wonder.

One main stair rose out of the hall, at its south-west corner, a curving stone

The fourteenth-century hall is the finest domestic hall to survive in Britain, and one of the very few to retain its central hearth. The tall Gothic windows and huge chestnut roof recall ecclesiastical buildings of the same period.

flight winding up an external tower with treads six feet long and so massive that you could still ride a horse up them. It led to the solar. This was a long room for the family with a central hooded fireplace and was probably unpartitioned. Clearly these two great rooms, the hall and solar, would no longer satisfy the new owners of Penshurst in the late fourteenth and early fifteenth centuries. They built an extension leading west from a corner of the solar, almost as large as the hall itself. For centuries it has been known as the Buckingham Building, after the Dukes of Buckingham who owned Penshurst from 1446 to 1521. But it must be earlier in date. One can attribute it either to Sir John Devereux (the owner from 1382 to 1393) or to the Duke of Bedford (1435–46), after whom it was first named as late as 1607. It has been so much altered that it is now impossible to fix its date or exact purpose. We cannot tell how many floors it held, nor how exactly it was divided by partitions. Nor do we know what other buildings were added to the hall in later mediaeval times. Around the house there were five or six turrets which may have resulted from Devereux's license to crenellate his house in 1392; and one reads in documents of the 'Great Stables' and the 'Great Tower', which suggest outbuildings which have disappeared. Certainly there must have been extensive accommodation by 1519, when the third Duke of Buckingham entertained King Henry VIII with great magnificence. The design of the buildings forming the south-west corner of the main courtyard indicates that it may have been one of Buckingham's extensions. If so, the plan of Penshurst was beginning to emerge before the manor was given to the Sidneys by King Edward VI in 1552.

Sir Philip Sidney, the poet and soldier, who was born at Penshurst in 1554. He owned the house for a few months, but at the age of 32 died of wounds received at the Battle of Zutphen.

However great the names that have so far been paraded, it is always with the Sidneys that Penshurst will be associated. They were the first owners to regard it as their home instead of a convenient and profitable Kentish annexe to other estates. They still own it four hundred years later, in the person of William Sidney, Viscount De L'Isle. The family produced sons and daughters who played great roles in the State, and by their grace and courage aroused affection as well as admiration, generation after generation. Contemporaries regarded one of them, Sir Philip Sidney, the poet, courtier, statesman and soldier, as the man by whom they would wish the whole Elizabethan age to be remembered. When he died aged thirty-two of wounds received at the Battle of Zutphen, Camden wrote of him: 'This is that Sidney who as Providence seems to have sent him into the world to give the present a specimen of the ancients, so it did on a sudden recall him and snatch him from us as more worthy of heaven than of earth!' Over two hundred years later Shelley, whose family was connected with the Sidneys, could write in his *Adonais*:

> *Sidney, as he fought*
> *And as he fell, and as he loved and lived,*
> *Sublimely mild, a spirit without spot.*

A room is still pointed out at Penshurst as the room where this paragon was born, and he spent much of his boyhood there. But he owned it for no more than five months between his father's death in May and his own in October, 1586, and he left no physical mark upon it. It was his father, Sir Henry Sidney,

*The range of mediaeval buildings seen from the
south. From left to right are the Buckingham
Building, the turret-staircase, the solar,
the Baron's Hall, and the garden tower.*

and his brother Robert who gave Penshurst its final form. All later changes were complementary. In the nineteenth century the cult of the antique coincided with loss of architectural self-confidence, and when later Sidneys restored or modified the house, they did so externally in the style which was contemporary with these two men. Internally they allowed themselves a little more licence in the Gothic tradition.

Sir Henry Sidney (1529–86) and his second son, Robert Sidney, later first Earl of Leicester, identified most of their work by tablets on outside walls, or by initials on rainwater-heads and on inside panelling. The sequence of their building or rebuilding is therefore fairly clear. It was probably in 1560–2, when the accounts record unusual activity by masons, carpenters and tile makers, 'working on my lord's work', that Sir Henry threw out the northern wing, linking it southwards with the Buckingham Building and westwards with one of the mediaeval towers, which he widened and heightened. Along the ground floor he inserted an open colonnade of seven arches, and added an octagonal turret of brick within which a beautiful oak staircase spirals up to the room where Sir Philip Sidney was, by tradition, born. Finally, in the last year of his life, 1585–6, he replaced the presumed mediaeval entrance by the King's Tower, which is still the main entrance from the park, setting it slightly askew, as his steward recorded, 'so that he might see clear through the porch and service corridor of the hall to the garden'.

The house was by this time virtually complete. Robert finished his father's entrance tower (the doors carry the initials of himself and his wife), built a new stable-block, and after some delay completed the Long Gallery in 1607, a building which his father probably started. This room is without doubt the loveliest in the house. The Elizabethan–Jacobean formula was followed with subtle variations. It runs along the upper storey of the southernmost wing, with unencumbered views over the garden and the park, and widens at the end into a panelled chamber formed from the first floor of another of the mediaeval towers. The central bay opposite the fireplace gives the gallery additional variety. It thus avoids the cigar-box lines of many such galleries, affording privacy at different points down its great length. It has a festive, summery quality; it is a room for music or flirtation; it is cool and light and demands to be filled with flowers. Below it is a second gallery, which the present Lord De L'Isle has cleared of clutter to re-form a nether-gallery which leads to the garden.

Penshurst, indeed, is one vast garden-house. As early as the written records begin, we read of the care which was given to the terracing, pools and cultivation of fruit-trees. The letters exchanged between Robert Sidney and his wife and agents are full of references to new plantings. You can see the result of it today in the marriage between house and garden, for both are still beautifully maintained. But Penshurst is a marriage between centuries too. F. S. Boas, Sir Philip Sidney's latest biographer, has summed him up as 'combining in himself some of the salient features of mediaevalism and of the Renaissance'. The same is true of his house. Its slim strong lines are the product of discipline and innovation, of clear intention and haphazard

The Long Gallery was completed in 1607, running the length of the upper storey of the southern wing. It is the most festive room in the house, and is hung with portraits of the Sidney family.

growth. Almost any one of its many façades reveals patchwork of a kind, so that the house as a whole can be read like an architectural textbook. But with what skill and love was it assembled and extended, and its decaying parts restored! If it is ever legitimate to attribute to stone and brick and glass and timber a character which is the sum of all its past inhabitants, the place to do so is at Penshurst. It is amusing to decipher its different periods, but the attempt must not be allowed to destroy the Arcadian quality of the whole. The search for information can render a house more factually intelligible but less truly understood. As Richard Church wrote of Penshurst, 'There is such a thing as too much longing for knowledge' of how it came to be what it is. In the end the house must speak for itself.

OPPOSITE *Penshurst slowly grew outwards from the original Hall (centre), to link it with one of the surrounding towers right) and the Buckingham Building (left). All this was completed by 1450, and still remains externally unchanged.*

OVERLEAF LEFT *The entrance front of Ightham Mote. The house is surrounded by a moat on all four sides, and bridges cross three of them. The water is fed by springs and remains constantly clear.*

OVERLEAF RIGHT *The Banqueting Hall at Haddon Hall, dating from the early fourteenth century, looking towards the Minstrels Gallery. The antlers have been there since the reign of Charles II.*

Oxburgh Hall
Norfolk

THE FIRST SIGHT OF OXBURGH from the road could raise the question whether it should have a place in this book at all: it is apparently a castle, not a house, with all the outward apparatus of fortification – a moat, battlements, arrow-slits and a vast turreted, machicolated gatehouse. A closer look makes clear that all these features, while certainly deriving from mediaeval castles, have undergone subtle changes. The moat is now crossed by a fixed bridge, not a drawbridge. The majority of the arrow-slits are so sited that no bowman could possibly have let fly from them at an enemy below. Nothing can ever have been dropped from the machicolations on the south side, for they are sealed by the original stone. The gatehouse does not frown, for it is a work of architecture, not primarily a work of defence: it is built of brick, not stone, and it is pierced on its most exposed side by two large and delicate windows.

Thus the whole building forms an extremely interesting illustration of how a great county family, itself adept at war and experienced in the treacherous ways of the fifteenth century, was feeling its way towards greater comfort and architectural elegance even at the cost of increased vulnerability to attack. Oxburgh was started by Sir Edmund Bedingfeld in 1482, three years before the Wars of the Roses came to an end. The defences would have kept marauding beggars out of the courtyard, but little more; they could not have resisted an organized attack for a single day. The military embellishments were largely decorative and the layout was designed for display, entertainment on a lavish scale, and the raising of large families. The proof of its domesticity is that the house has been occupied as the home of the Bedingfelds for nearly five hundred years with scarcely a break and no basic change to its structure. Its claim to be a superb work of architecture has been endorsed by one critic after another. 'One of the noblest specimens of the domestic architecture of the fifteenth century,' wrote the elder Pugin, 'The finest building of its generation,' said Avray Tipping. And in his *Pattern of English Building* Clifton-Taylor calls it 'one of England's most enchanting pieces of architectural pageantry'.

Attention is first focused on the great tower, not only because it almost monopolizes the view from the entrance gates, but because it is by far the most striking feature of the house and the least altered. This splendid building rises

OPPOSITE *The main entrance to Oxburgh Hall, seen from the road between the gate-piers, each surmounted by the Bedingfeld eagle.*

Sir Henry Bedingfeld, who was entrusted by
Mary Tudor with the custody of the future
Queen Elizabeth I. Oxburgh has belonged to
the Bedingfeld family ever since it was built.

from the moat like a cliff from the sea. It is formed by two octagonal turrets joined by a curtain wall. The turrets are placed close together to emphasize the height of the tower, and they are topped by doubly serrated battlements which have the majesty of tiaras. At intervals horizontal brick mouldings are slung like lace round the shafts, and the turret windows, thrown into deep shadow by their depth, are black caverns compared to the sparkle of the central lights. The tower is not quite symmetrical, for the windows are larger and more widely spaced in the left-hand turret than in the right, and a projection for the garderobes is attached to one side. But it gives the impression of symmetry because the skyline is perfectly balanced. Who could doubt, after examining this façade in reality or in a photograph, that its builders were acutely aware of the dramatic effect of what they were doing?

The reverse side of the gatehouse is treated quite differently. Here the turrets stop short of the parapet, and two watch-towers, corbelled outwards at the angles, carry the eye upwards. There is no main window on this side, only a large square sundial set in the wall between the turret tops and a stone achievement of the Bedingfeld arms below. You are now within the square central courtyard. The great hall originally stood opposite the gatehouse, and two-storeyed apartments ran round the other three sides. It is a place for the family, not the stranger; for stamping hooves, not the soft pad of motor tyres: but as you drive across the bridge, under the tower and into the courtyard, it is impossible not to sense something of the exhilaration which generations of Bedingfelds felt on arriving home. One might expect to feel shut in by these great walls, towers and moat. But Oxburgh is an outward-looking house, for all its remoteness and seclusion. Its brick is so mellow, its external windows so numerous and large, its garden and surrounding countryside so friendly, that even the moat appears from within as nothing more formidable than an encircling lake.

The same impression is given by the interior of the tower, usually the grimmest part of a castellated mansion. There are only two main rooms within it, each occupying the full breadth and width of the first and second storeys, and known respectively as the King's Room and the Queen's Room ever since Henry VII's visit to Oxburgh in 1497. The word 'room' seems inadequate: one calls them instinctively 'chambers', for they have great dignity achieved by apparently artless means – plain whitewashed or mottle-brick walls, fireplaces with four-centred arches, window embrasures as large as small oratories formed from the turrets on both sides, high timber ceilings and floors covered most appropriately with mats of woven rush. The Queen's Room is furnished simply, but the play of light on the walls and ribbed roofs of the octagonal chambers makes it an enchanting room just to stand in. The King's Room below is slightly more elaborate, and next door to it is Oxburgh's greatest single possession, the bed-hangings and coverlet embroidered by Mary Queen of Scots and Bess of Hardwick during the Queen's imprisonment. In these two rooms there is a lesson for the architect or decorator of any age. Their simple structural shapes, receding and advancing in three dimensions, now curved, now rectilinear, create a feeling of liveliness

and welcome which could scarcely be bettered.

The staircase which links the two tower-rooms and rises to the leads is an astonishing feat of virtuosity. It is a tight spiral based on a geometrical design of such ingenuity that it is as difficult to discover exactly how it was done as it is for a shrimp inside a Nautilus shell to make out the secret of its convolutions. The only part of the staircase which is at rest are the flat treads: the soffit (underside) of the steps swings upwards, sweeping from concave to convex and back again with a smooth rolling motion that stands the bricks virtually on their heads and seems to presage imminent collapse: but it has stood the passage of five centuries. This is true of all the brickwork at Oxburgh. It has worn marvellously, even when exposed eighty foot up on the turret tops. The Norfolk bricklayers of 1480 have had no rivals since. To take a single example, the bricks forming the corners of the turrets have been cut by hand in five separate planes, none of them at right-angles, and the whole building must contain many hundreds of thousands of bricks shaped in this fashion.

Oxburgh retains its original ground-plan and main structure. But there have been many internal changes and one act of vandalism. In 1775 Sir Richard Bedingfeld pulled down the Tudor hall and Great Chamber opposite

OPPOSITE One side of the great brick house, with the entrance tower on the right, and a well-integrated nineteenth-century tower on the left.

The King's Room on the central floor of the tower. According to tradition it was occupied by Henry VII on his visit in 1487. The four-poster bed bears the date 1675.

the gateway, and left the south side of the courtyard open to the moat. The gap was closed again in the nineteenth century by a passageway, and two low towers were raised at the south-west and south-east angles in the eighteenth and nineteenth centuries respectively. In about 1880 external corridors were added round the inside of the courtyard. These additions have not done as much damage to the appearance of the house as the loss of the Great Hall – though one would wish the corridors away – because the restorations of the last two centuries were usually carried out in a brick which fairly matched the Tudor originals. The dreadful consequences of using machine-made, mutton-red brick can be seen in the Victorian surrounds of some of the windows, and the design of them suggests that the Bedingfeld of the day threw at the west front every Tudor device that he could find in the architectural encyclopaedia. But nothing can dim the splendour of the old walls in which they are set, and nothing in the whole of architecture could be crisper than the fall of the angle-buttresses into the clear water of the moat.

Oxburgh survived, but only just. The staunch Catholic faith of the Bedingfelds led them into acts of desperate courage and acute distress. Three times the house was nearly abandoned for scrap: once after the Civil War when it was left by Cromwell's soldiers ransacked and partly burning; again in the eighteenth century, when the family fortunes were drained to keep it in repair; and finally in our own times. In 1951 the heir to the property was forced by financial difficulties to sell the estate to a development company. It was the first time that Oxburgh had passed out of the hands of the Bedingfelds for five hundred years, Three months later the company put up the house for auction, and the only prospective buyer was a demolition firm that intended to pull it down. On the very morning of the sale, Lady Bedingfeld, who has lived here for seventy years, found the necessary money to buy it back. When the name of the purchaser was announced, the audience burst into spontaneous applause.

An air-view of Oxburgh Hall, showing the moat which surrounds the house on all four sides. It is crossed, in one place only, by the bridge which leads under the great entrance tower.

Compton Wynyates
Warwickshire

THE FIRST AND LASTING IMPRESSION of the house is its colour. An absence of twelve hours, or even a night spent within its walls, is enough to blur the memory of its startling appearance from outside, so that on returning the next morning it comes as a renewed surprise to find that something so old can glow so richly. It does not even need the sun to bring out the mottled raspberry of the brick. The bricks contain it. But not only the brick, for the stone tiles of the roof and the two half-timbered gables on the entrance side add a dash of grey and black which together with the surrounding trees and lawns turn the whole composition into a scattering of rose-petals in a glade. The second impression is of its situation. Cupped on all but one side in a tight circle of wooded hills, no great house is more deliberately lost in the flounces of the countryside. You only see it for the first time when you have approached within two or three hundred yards and a stab of colour suddenly pierces the canopy of leaves. But, though secluded, the house does not feel hemmed in. The water of the moat leads the eye northwards to the only gap in the hills (the 'wind-gate', which is one possible derivation of the name) over which stands, appropriately, a windmill; and the slopes of the valley have been flattened and terraced to form yew-filled gardens and grass walks which upholster the house on all sides.

The third impression is of its irregularity. This is not to say that the house is shapeless, for it is tightly knit on a roughly square plan, and there are no excrescences to spoil its compactness, vertically or horizontally. But it is not 'architected'. It grew new limbs as convenience demanded and the site made possible, and in no part of the house is there any attempt at symmetry. The gables are of unequal height and pitch, more than forty twisted chimneys settle inconsequently all over the roofs, turrets of different shapes and a curtain-wing were added on available ledges, and even the main east and west roofs were stepped higher behind than in front so that from a short distance one appears to extend the slope of the other. Compton Wynyates is in fact the most glorious of Tudor jumbles. It is as if little models of different parts of different buildings from all over the country had been assembled in this one place and blocked together to form a house. A knowledge of how it came to look like this, and of the events that happened there, immeasurably increases its interest, but the immediate impact made by the house is that here,

*The south front seen from above the topiary
garden, still known as the Best Garden. The
large window in the centre is that of the chapel
built in about 1515. Above the house stands the
windmill, associated with the name 'wind-gate'
or Wynyates.*

obviously, is an expression of a native English style that had taken many hundreds of years to mature and was as yet unaffected by the neo-classical influence that was soon to sweep the country from Italy and France.

The Comptons, who climbed the social scale through knighthood, barony and earldom to the present Marquisate of Northampton, have lived on this site since the early thirteenth century. The only certain trace of their first manor-house is the moat, which encircled the present house until the mid-seventeenth century. The position of the moat raises a problem. Today three of its stunted arms lie round the garden to the north of the house, and lawns fill the wide fosses by which it was once continued round the entire rectangle in which Compton Wynyates lies. Either the mediaeval house must have been almost double the size of that which we see today; or the moat was extended to include its garden; or the manor stood within the three existing arms and the new house was built alongside it, the moat being prolonged to include both the old site and the new; or the original entrance was on the north side and outbuildings occupied the area of the present garden. Of the four possibilities the last seems the most likely. But if the mediaeval entrance was on the north front, this was one of the fundamental changes of plan which Edmund Compton made when he decided to rebuild the manor during his ownership between 1481 and 1493. He switched the entrance and the outbuildings to the west, and enclosed the latter by another moat, perhaps dry, crossed by a second drawbridge. His home was therefore still patently a castle, and its fortification is the main argument for a late fifteenth-century date, for which no documentary evidence survives. The core of the present house, including the four wings around the internal courtyard and the Big Hall, was his; and we owe to him the extravagant choice of brick in a stone-country, and the grey roofs and the ceilings of carved timber which run round the north and west wings.

That it was a beautiful house as well as a strong one there can be no doubt. But Edmund's son, Sir William Compton, invested it with its present pageantry. It was he who built the chapel, the entrance porch and the towers at the four angles, and he who embellished the interior with bay-windows, stained glass and the roofing of the hall. He took some of his materials from Fulbroke Castle near Warwick, a decayed mansion dating from 1435, so that in effect he added an extra half-century to the date of his father's house. Later generations were equally solicitous of its Tudor character. In about 1730 the fifth Earl of Northampton added in the same general style a wing between the two corner towers on the east front, and over a hundred years later Sir Digby Wyatt was commissioned to Gothicize the Georgian windows and to build a new staircase. None of these improvements have spoiled the Tudor work, while greatly adding to the convenience of the house. It remains in essentials the house which the two Comptons, father and son, built in thirty years of the reigns of Henry VII and Henry VIII.

They were a remarkable family. On Edmund's death in 1493 he left his eleven-year-old son a ward of the Crown, and the boy was appointed page to Prince Henry, aged two, later Henry VIII. The friendship between King and

ABOVE *Henry* VIII's *room, in which Elizabeth* I, *James* I *and Charles* I *also slept. The ceiling, dating from 1625, incorporates the monograms of all four monarchs.*

RIGHT *The Big Hall, looking towards the Minstrels Gallery. The roof is fifteenth-century, and the linenfold panelling of the screen dates from the reign of Henry* VIII.

OPPOSITE *The entrance porch. Over the archway are the royal arms of England surmounted by a crown inscribed* DOM REX HENRICUS OCTAV. *Sir William Compton was a close friend of Henry* VIII.

courtier was to last until William's early death in 1528. As companions-in-arms in war and tourneys, as master and emissary in diplomacy and politics, as constant partners in the hunting-field and banqueting-hall, their relationship is all the more remarkable for having been deepened by the passage of years instead of poisoned by it. King Henry knighted William Compton for gallantry at the Battle of Tournai (1512) and granted him the exceptional privilege of adding to his coat-of-arms the Royal Lion of England. The King stayed at Compton Wynyates on more than one occasion, as did

47

Queen Elizabeth I, James I and Charles I, and it is next to certain that they all slept in the room still known as Henry VIII's Room, which includes their four monograms in the plasterwork of the ceiling. There is no place where the visitor can better savour the atmosphere of Compton Wynyates than in this room. For not only is this simple chamber in a comparatively modest house enriched by the memory of the four monarchs, but from its windows the inner courtyard is seen to its greatest advantage, ruddy with ageing brick, glinting with diamond panes and as peaceful as a college quadrangle.

But Compton was also the scene of battle. In the Civil War the second Earl of Northampton and his family were undivided in their loyalty to the Crown. The father and his three eldest sons (the fourth, aged thirteen, crying in indignation that he was not allowed to share the dangers with his brothers) fought in the Battle of Edgehill, six miles from the house, and the three youths were all knighted on the battlefield. The Earl was killed in the Battle of Hopton Heath in 1643 in the moment of victory, having, when offered his life by the Roundheads, 'scorned to take quarter from such base rogues and rebels'. The six sons survived constant fighting until the Royalist cause was lost, but the house itself suffered. In 1644 Compton Wynyates was captured by the Roundheads after a two-day siege, and an attempt to recapture it six months later was unsuccessful, perhaps because the Comptons, sallying out from Royalist Banbury, did not want to press home the attack to the point of utterly destroying the house which they loved so well. At the end of the war the family went into exile, and the moat was filled in by order of Parliament. The house was kept in sufficiently good repair during the two succeeding centuries for its main structure to have survived almost unimpaired. That the Northamptons lived mainly in their other house, Castle Ashby, saved Compton Wynyates, like Haddon Hall, from excessive modernization. When the sixth Marquess came to write the history of his family in 1929, he dated it from Castle Ashby, but entitled his book *History of the Comptons of Compton Wynyates*. As the Germans would say, it is Compton that they regard as their *Stammsitz*.

Nobody visiting the house could remain for long unaware of its strong sense of continuity. It is not only the scars of use and misuse which remind one of its past, the wearing of steps, paving-stones and banister-rails to which the present-day visitor innocently contributes by placing his foot and hand in exactly the same positions as came naturally to the occupants and soldiery of nearly five centuries; but the very structure of the place, which combined sturdiness with pride and elegance in a manner which we can admire but cannot imitate; and the peace which has descended on the house, a peace which its earlier owners neither sought nor found.

The Vyne
Hampshire

THE NAME IS OF GREAT ANTIQUITY. It occurs in a deed as early as 1268, and anyone who dares can take it further back to the *Vindomis* of the second-century Antonine Itinerary. This 'house-of-wine' could have been a private villa or an inn on the route from Winchester to Reading, and relics found in the garden support the theory of a Roman origin. The Vyne, however, does not need to draw on archaeology to confirm its reputation. It is a composition of the sixteenth, seventeenth and eighteenth centuries, of which each has contributed something of startling novelty for its time. That a house so gentle and apparently so traditional should have been the scene of architectural experiment comes as a surprise. That each period should blend so happily with the next is a tribute to the taste of the two families with which it will always be associated – the families of Sandys and Chute.

The house is basically Tudor. Its walls of rose-coloured brick, patterned unobtrusively with diamond diapering, proclaim it at once as a building of the early sixteenth century. It was built between 1500 and 1520 by the first Lord Sandys, Lord Chamberlain to Henry VIII, and he entertained his King there on three separate occasions. On the site, according to Leland, there had been a 'no very great or sumptuous manor place . . . and [Sandys] so translated it and augmented it that it became one of the most princely houses in goodly building in all Hampshire'. Nothing of the mediaeval house remains, unless Sandys used some of its materials, and when he came to build his own he adopted a style which owed little to any predecessor, except perhaps to the earliest period of Hampton Court. Because the Vyne was later associated with more famous men, Sandys has not always been given his due share of credit for this lovely building. For its age, it was revolutionary. The moat, which Leland mentions as surrounding the earlier house, was discarded. Tall windows were symmetrically arranged across both main fronts. The house faced outwards, with no internal courtyard. The hall did not occupy the whole width of the house, but only half of it, and it did not rise to the full height of the roof (though the point is still in dispute) but appears to have been ceilinged at first-floor level. At each corner, as eighteenth-century pictures show, stood a sturdy tower, rising an extra storey to give the building a rigidity and balance that one can describe without anachronism as architectural. Sandys extended its area by a 'faire base-court' (again Leland's phrase) which reached within a few yards of the present lake, and on the entrance front there was a forecourt, presumably with a gatehouse in its centre. Thus Sandys' inventiveness anticipated by fifty years or more an arrangement which became normal in the early years of Queen Elizabeth. The catalogue is still not concluded. He constructed one of the very first long galleries to be found in any English country-house. He broke up his main fronts and wings into small parlours and bedrooms, which on one Elizabethan occasion were able to accommodate the French ambassador and four hundred members of his suite. His only omissions were those for which he cannot be blamed: there were no sanitary arrangements except some primitive water channels; and there were no corridors. The first deficiency has been remedied, but so well was the house planned for convenience and comfort that none of his successors have found it necessary to make good the second.

Although Shakespeare in his *Henry VIII* puts into Sandys'' mouth the self-deprecatory words 'I am an honest country Lord', he displayed in his house a quite remarkable flair for the work of contemporary foreign artists. One can attribute it partly to his proximity to the King, than whom few English monarchs have been less insular in their tastes, and partly to his long sojourns abroad in the King's service. At the Vyne there are four outstanding examples of such work, executed either by foreigners directly or by Englishmen working under Continental influence. Three of them are in the chapel: the stained glass is Flemish, probably imported direct from Liège; the lovely choir-stalls, Gothic in conception, incorporate lively Renaissance motifs; and the encaustic tiles are attributed by Bernard Rackham to the Antwerp workshop of Guido de Savino from Urbino. The fourth example is in the Oak Gallery. As a room it can be rather disappointing for one of the most famous rooms in Britain, since its great length is not balanced by window-bays of compensating depth and its single fireplace is not enough to break the monotony of the opposite wall. But one's attention is immediately caught by the four rows of linenfold panelling, extending from floor to ceiling along each side, making some four hundred panels in all. They are ornamented with the badges, crests or initials of the King, Sandys himself, his relations and his friends, with a joyful fecundity of invention unparalleled in any other wainscoting in the country. Unfortunately the panels were overpainted at some period in a warm chocolate-brown, and it has been found too dangerous to the woodwork and too expensive to remove it. The crispness of the carving is only slightly smudged by this outrage. It is English work and English in feeling: but one panel above a side-door departs from the general style of the remainder to illustrate two *putti* supporting the Royal Arms – a device so free and enchanting, so remarkable a break with Gothic tradition, that one begins to wonder whether one has strayed into the wrong country in the wrong half of the century.

William Sandys died in 1540, leaving behind him a beautiful house that few of his descendants wished to alter. It was sold by the sixth Lord Sandys in 1653 to Chaloner Chute, Speaker of the House of Commons during the

Commonwealth. Chute's name has suffered an undeserved eclipse. The tributes paid to him on his early death in 1659 leave no doubt that he was regarded by contemporaries as one of the most outstanding men of his age, and that his personal charm and integrity acted as political stabilizers in a period of exceptional unrest. He made several important alterations to the Vyne. He swept away the courtyards, back and front. He replaced the mullioned windows by others in rectangular stone frames. And he commissioned John Webb, the disciple of Inigo Jones, to erect a Corinthian portico against the north front. It was a bold innovation, the first portico of its kind to be added to a private house. Seen from across the lake, it seems to stamp the house as Palladian, but it was erected nearly fifty years before Lord Burlington was born. Its cleanliness of line is slightly spoiled by abrupt side-openings, which are rectangular and bricked instead of arched and plastered, and it is tempting to suppose that the portico was never quite finished as Webb intended. In contrast, the lovely little garden-house or pigeon-loft in the form of a Greek cross with a central dome, also by Webb, is a perfect seventeenth-century pavilion that links the Tudor phase of the house to its second transformation a hundred years later.

The Tudor north front, to which John Webb added in 1654 the earliest classical portico in any English country house. On the left is the chapel with the two blind windows inserted in the nineteenth century.

The Speaker's descendant was John Chute, the friend of Horace Walpole. That he should be thus remembered, and not Walpole as Chute's friend, is due to the richness of Walpole's literary testament and the fact that he was born the son of a Prime Minister. For, of the two, Chute was the greater innovator. Walpole himself admitted it. He wrote to Horace Mann in 1747, 'If I were to say all I think of Chute's immense honesty, his sense, his worth, his knowledge and his humanity, you would think that I was writing a dedication.' For thirty-two years Chute had lived abroad, mostly in Italy, and only inherited the Vyne unexpectedly in 1754, when the last of his many brothers died childless. The house could not have fallen into more fitting hands. He respected the work of Sandys, but only on second or third thoughts, for he was an architect of the Strawberry Hill school – indeed, after Walpole, its leader – and he chose to have himself painted with an elevation in his hand for the Gothicizing of the entire exterior. As it was, Chute and Walpole between them (with the irreverent jocularity their correspondence reveals) Strawberried

ABOVE *The Ante-Chapel, redecorated in the Strawberry Hill style under the influence of Horace Walpole. The main door leads through to the chapel.*

OPPOSITE *One of the entrances to the Vyne. The stone eagle was given to John Chute by his friend Horace Walpole. The brickwork is Tudor, but the windows and doorways were refashioned in the seventeenth century.*

OVERLEAF *The entrance front of Compton Wynyates.*

52

OPPOSITE *The upper storey of the staircase at the Vyne, built by John Chute to replace the Tudor hall. The galleries flanked by Corinthian columns are a brilliantly theatrical device in the confined space available.*

PREVIOUS PAGE TOP *Longleat in 1671, a painting by Jan Siberechts. The entrance front has remained virtually unchanged, but the forecourt was removed, and the stables to the left were replaced by Wyattville's huge block behind.*

BOTTOM *Approximately the same view photographed today.*

RIGHT *The foot of John Chute's classical staircase, begun about 1765.*

only one room, the Ante-Chapel, and with its tawdry fretwork and dull colouring it cannot be counted a success. But for his major alteration Chute switched to a style of classical purity. He constructed an ice-cool staircase rising from just inside the front door in a series of columned galleries. The whole is evident at a glance, but the ingenuity of its different levels and openings, all contrived within a minimal space, make it, as Walpole himself observed, 'theatrical' and almost playful. Never was simplicity developed with so dramatic a touch. It would make an ideal setting for a children's charade, but at the same time it has grace and importance, and from no angle – and every angle was carefully considered – do its rosettes and pretty columns degenerate into frivolity.

In the series of living-rooms on the ground floor Chute was content with a more reposeful habitableness. His red damask, bought in Italy in about 1760, created a neutral background to the Strawberry Committee's endless conversations, and fortunately they did not tamper with Sandys' Chapel Parlour with its soothing linenfold and Tudor portraits, which is still the most pleasant room in the house. But Chute did add to the chapel itself a 'Tomb Chamber' to the memory of his ancestor, the Speaker. In it he placed a recumbent effigy of such indolent grace that the Speaker might be reclining in a hayfield instead of on a cenotaph constructed a hundred years after his death. That the sculptor of this superb figure is still in doubt – Thomas Bankes, say some; Thomas Carter, say others – is not untypical of the Vyne, but whichever it turns out to be will have established an undying reputation by this single work.

There is no need to go beyond John Chute's death in 1776 to describe the Vyne as it appears today. All that was most worthwhile had been done by then, and nothing that was still to come did much damage. The Chutes were not as progenitive as they were imaginative, and the house slipped sideways through cousins and nephews to keep the Chute name alive until 1956, when Sir Charles Chute bequeathed the house, its contents and the estate to the National Trust. It is still one of the most perfect of English houses. In spite of its size and richness it has a certain modesty of character, which is the product of linenfold, tapestry, coloured glass, Chippendale, portraits, flowers and a sound roof on wide brick walls.

The 'Tomb chamber', containing the monument of Speaker Chaloner Chute in Carrara marble, commissioned by John Chute in 1775. The effigy is probably by Thomas Carter.

Longleat
House
Wiltshire

THE FIRST SIGHT OF THE HOUSE is from a mile away and several hundred feet above it. The approach drive from the Warminster road swings through parkland to the crest of a wooded hill, and then suddenly, through columns of grey trees, you see the house standing on a plateau of closely cropped grass, and below it, a chain of lakes formed from the long *leat* or watercourse which gave the house its name. The park surrounds it in silence. On all but one side the hills create a bowl in which the house rests, but the undulations of the countryside are so harmonious, so artfully furnished with trees, bridges and avenues, with no walls or hedges to divide road from grass, grass from woods, that one can be forgiven for describing Longleat first in terms of its setting.

It comes as no surprise to learn that we owe it to Lancelot Brown, whose reputation had reached its zenith when Lord Weymouth commissioned him in 1757 to remodel the park. Brown swept away the elaborate gardens seen in the Kip engravings, and created the woodlands, lakes and vistas over the apparently natural countryside. Already by 1760 Mrs Delaney could write ecstatically: 'We got to Longleat! There is not much alteration in the house, but the gardens are no more! They are succeeded by a fine lawn, a serpentine river, wooded hills, gravel paths meandering round a shrubbery, all modernized by the ingenious and much sought-after Mr Brown!' Not everyone shared Mrs Delaney's enthusiasm. Lord Weymouth was criticized for doing away with the *parterres* and clipped alleys of his ancestors, and Longleat was often quoted as the most glaring example of Brown's 'vandalism'. But in its present maturity, the landscaping of the park is seen as a work of art complementary to the house itself.

The builder of Longleat was Sir John Thynne, a faithful adjutant in war and peace of the Lord Protector, Duke of Somerset, by whom he was knighted on the battlefield of Pinkie (1547) while his wounds were still bleeding. Somerset was executed in 1552, and Thynne shared in his master's disgrace to the extent of spending two years in the Tower of London and paying a £6,000 fine. On his release he returned to his Wiltshire estates and until his death in 1580 applied himself almost exclusively to the building of his house. A contemporary portrait of him at the age of fifty-one leaves only one aspect of his character unexplained. Hand on sword-hilt, his stance proud and aggressive,

his glance betraying the hot temper with which he ruled his army of workmen, one would scarcely have guessed that this was the man who created the most perfectly classical house of the early English Renaissance. From whom did he obtain his knowledge, his taste, his eye for foreign detail? Part of it could have come from the Lord Protector, who reconstructed Syon and built Somerset House, which incorporated much French ornamentation. Two Frenchmen, Allen Maynard and Adrian Gaunt, and the Englishmen Robert Smythson and William Spicer, later Surveyor of the Queen's Works, are known to have been employed at Longleat for long periods at a time, and they must have contributed their own ideas. But the records still preserved in the house make it quite clear that Sir John Thynne was not only the driving force, but was capable of conceiving startling architectural innovations. For instance, he wrote to Spicer in 1557, 'All stairs are to ryse above the house and are to be tiped [? given tops]; four to have little stairs wonne from the roof so they may serve as banketting houses.' What he meant by the last phrase is not at all clear, for there is scarcely room in these domed turrets for a dolls' tea-party, let alone a banquet, but in this brief note there is sufficient evidence to attribute to Sir John himself one of the most original and effective features of the house, and he carried it through to completion with typical audacity and persistence.

The huge cube of Longleat, like so many other houses of this date including Syon, was raised on the site of an earlier priory. One of the two inner courts may rest upon the foundations of the monastic cloister, for several coffins of the Black Canons were discovered here during reconstructions of the early nineteenth century. But if one excepts the Great Hall, there is nothing mediaeval about the house itself. The exterior was composed of symmetrical units of Elizabethan windows forming bold bays and recesses on a scale that only Lord Burghley was attempting elsewhere. The proportions of the façades would be strong rather than graceful were it not for the incorporation of Italianate motifs of astonishing maturity for so early a period. The three classical orders, Doric below, Ionic in the middle and Corinthian at the level of the top storey, were superimposed between the windows across the whole width of each façade. Below the windows were set circular recesses for busts of Roman emperors. Thick cornices were sandwiched between the floors, and a balustrade runs the whole length of the flat roof, crowned most effectively since 1685 by four baroque statues. In 1575 the house had been erected as far as the top of the second storey, by which time construction had been in progress for at least twelve years, interrupted by a fire in 1567 which was not brought under control for four hours. The top storey may have been added after 1580 by Sir John's son, for there is no mention of a Corinthian order in the records, only of 'Dorrick and Yonk', the master-mason's approximation to Doric and Ionic, which he described in stone better than in his spelling.

The second great innovation of Longleat was its plan. Hitherto, houses had been built either to the E-plan, the two wings and the porch forming the horizontal strokes of the E, or to the courtyard plan, with the main rooms facing inwards. Sir John Thynne's house has two inner courtyards, but they are light-wells more than architectural features in their own right, and every

A view through the ornamental stonework of the roof, looking towards the baroque statues placed there in 1685.

The entrance front of Longleat, completed
in about 1580. It is the only truly
classical house of the Elizabethan period,
incorporating the three classic orders,
Doric, Ionic and Corinthian, one above
the other.

The Great Hall, the least-changed part
of the Elizabethan house. The fireplace
dates from the late sixteenth century, and
the hunting scenes were painted by
Wootton.

main room looks outwards to the park. The original floor-plans, which Sir John sent to Lord Burghley for his comments, show that the north side of the house was closed only by a wall. Conceivably this wing was destroyed by the 1567 fire before it was completed, or its building was prevented by Sir John's death. But in the early nineteenth century Wyatville added on the fourth side a careful imitation of the other three fronts, thus completing what was probably Thynne's original intention.

Unfortunately it is not possible to visualize the appearance of the interior in the sixteenth century, since in three separate bursts of energy and affluence, successive Lords Weymouth (the Thynnes acquired the title in the reign of Charles II) totally transformed the internal structure of the house and the decoration of the rooms. Apart from the hall and cellars none of them contain any original Elizabethan features. Even in the maids' bedrooms the old fireplaces were ripped out and replaced. It is almost equally sad that the seventeenth and eighteenth-century renovations should have gone the same way as the Elizabethan. Only one great room survives from that period – Bishop Ken's library on the top floor. Thomas Ken (1637–1711), Bishop of Bath and Wells, was befriended by the first Viscount Weymouth after falling foul of James II and William and Mary, and was given this room in which to house his fine collection of books and spend a life of study and contemplation, Bishop Ken's Library, as it is still called, runs the whole length of the east front. It is shaped like a long Elizabethan gallery, but beautifully modified by projecting bays filled with leather-bound books, globes, pictures and early scientific instruments.

Between 1801 and 1811, Thomas Thynne, second Marquess of Bath, employed Sir Jeffry Wyatville to remodel the interior once again. At exactly the same time his uncle James Wyatt was performing the same service for Wilton, and both nephew and uncle made use of the identical technique of attaching corridors to all four sides of the inner courtyard to provide better access from room to room. At Wilton it was more skilfully done that at Longleat, for Wyatt made charming cloisters of his corridors, while Wyatville seems to have been quite unconcerned by their bleak appearance seen across the courtyard. He further added a huge central staircase to replace an earlier one attributed to Wren. But in compensation, he was responsible for two excellent features at Longleat, the north wing already mentioned, and the stable block which reproduces the spirit of the Elizabethan building so faithfully.

Finally, in 1860, the fourth Marquess, on his return from the Grand Tour, imported to Longleat a team of Italian craftsmen who Italianized the state-rooms beyond recognition. The workmanship is of superb quality, but its richness in no way compensates for the loss of the gentler native idiom which it replaced. When one recalls that Sir John Thynne employed at Longleat a 'connynge plasterer' whose work was so excellent that Sir William Cavendish enquired whether he might borrow him for Chatsworth (a request that was probably granted), one snaps one's fingers in irritation at the careful ceiling panels ('after Veronese') and gilded cornices of the Italians. Nevertheless,

Bishop Ken's library on the top floor of Longleat. Thomas Ken was Bishop of Bath and Wells in the late seventeenth century, and the room still contains his incomparable collection of books.

nobody could deny these rooms' magnificence, and they are filled with works of art and family portraits of high quality. In several of them, particularly the Saloon, the proportions are the same as those of Sir John Thynne's original house, and for that reason alone they can give the visitor great pleasure.

Longleat under the care of the present Lord Bath has become one of the most-visited houses in the country. Even if it were closed and empty, its incomparable setting and the beauty of its four palatial façades would still place it among the chief architectural glories of England. But Longleat is not a shell. Part of it is still lived in by Lord Weymouth, Lord Bath's son, and the grandest rooms are open daily to the public. In other corners there are hidden reserves, among them Bishop Ken's library, in which this description of the house was written.

Sulgrave
Manor
Northamptonshire

THIS MANOR-HOUSE WAS ALREADY MUCH DILAPIDATED by the end of the eighteenth century, and it was only because of the sturdiness of its construction that it was still standing as a common farm-house a hundred years later. Why then does it merit inclusion in a book about the great houses of Britain? There are three reasons. It is an excellent example of the smaller houses of the sixteenth century, extended in the eighteenth; it has been restored and furnished since 1914 with more taste and skill than can have been applied to any comparable building in the country; and it was built and inhabited by the direct ancestors of George Washington, the first President of the United States.

Sulgrave, moreover, is a very charming house. It is separated from the surrounding farmlands and village by a garden which is partly based on Elizabethan patterns but is planted with many shrubs and flowers that the Elizabethans never knew. The grey limestone of its walls and stone-tiled roof set it apart from the humbler thatched cottages of its estate without saddling it with an arrogance to which its builders never aspired. Its rooms reflect in miniature the best of two centuries of the English domestic arts. To the student of architecture it is a textbook of early methods of house-construction. To the historian it is a symbol of the past which the English share with the Americans. And, as if this were not enough, Sulgrave is a perfect illustration of how a house should be shown to the public. Scarcely a guard-rope, a notice or a drugget carpet mars the interior, and in their place we have bowls of beautifully arranged flowers, chairs that could be sat upon and beds that could be slept in, a kitchen fit to serve a banquet, and an absence of fuss that is a standing lesson to every decorator and housewife.

General George Washington was not particularly interested in his English ancestry, and he had never heard of Sulgrave. But he recorded a family tradition that 'they came from the north of England'. He was right. The Washingtons stemmed from Washington, originally Wessington, a village in County Durham, where they were to be found at the end of the twelfth century, and it is this village that ultimately gave its name to the capital of the western world. From there they moved to Lancashire in the early fourteenth century. The builder of Sulgrave Manor, Lawrence Washington, migrated to

The south front. The porch and the wing
to the right of it are all that remain of
Lawrence Washington's original house.
They contain the Great Hall on the
ground floor and the Great Chamber
above it. The left-hand wing was rebuilt
in the 1920s.

The arms of the Washington family in the spandrel of the entrance door. The theme of stars and stripes is supposed to have been the inspiration of the national flag of the United States.

Northamptonshire in about 1530 and made a small fortune as a wool-merchant in London and Northampton (of which he was twice Mayor) and later as a member of a sheep-raising partnership in the neighbourhood of Sulgrave. He was wealthy enough to buy the manor from the Crown in 1539 on the dissolution of the Priory of St Andrew at Northampton, to which it had belonged from at least the time of Henry I. He built the present house soon afterwards and completed it in about 1560. His son Robert added to it sufficient rooms to house his fifteen children by two successive wives. The house was sold to Robert's nephew, Lawrence Makepeace in 1610, and it again passed by sale from the Makepeaces to the Plants in 1659, and from the Plants to the Hodges in 1673.

The descent of the house is complicated, and need not concern us in detail; but the Washington line is quite clear. Colonel John Washington, a great-great-grandson of Lawrence, the builder of Sulgrave, emigrated to Virginia for business reasons in 1656, and he was the great-grandfather of the President, who was born in 1732. Thus George Washington was the direct descendant in the seventh generation of the Lawrence who built the house. In the late nineteenth century the tenant-farmer of Sulgrave would point out a Victorian bedstead in the Great Chamber as the bed in which the President was born. His pocket may have benefited more from the fiction than his reputation. But the connection is there all the same.

Compact though the manor is in its setting and general style, it is only partly the house which Lawrence built, but the part that has survived is the heart of the house, with its original entrance porch, Great Hall and Great Chamber. An east wing which extended over the present rose-garden has disappeared, and a west wing by which it was further lengthened on the other

The Great Chamber on the first floor. The Elizabethan four-poster bed came from Battle Abbey in Sussex.

side was also demolished at some period in the eighteenth century. This curtailment of the house was to some extent compensated by the addition of a north wing at right-angles to the main house by John Hodges in about 1700 and the partial rebuilding of the west wing by Sir Reginald Blomfield in 1930. In 1914 Sulgrave had been acquired and was later refurnished by Anglo-American subscriptions 'as a centre from which sentiments of friendship and goodwill between the British and American peoples will forever radiate'. Thus, if falsely sentimental associations are to be avoided, it is as important to understand the growth of the house as the descent of the family. Sulgrave is of three periods, Elizabethan, Queen Anne and the twentieth century, and only the first has any connection with the Washington family itself.

The house was never grand. The display of Queen Elizabeth's arms over the porch, their supporters repeated in plaster within it, was a loyal convention, not an assumption of a greater dignity than its builder ever earned or claimed. The hall is a lovely room, which owes more to its fine proportions and solid masonry and woodwork than to any elaboration of its detail. With its carefully chosen furniture of the period it must look very like the room in which Lawrence and his wife Amee entertained their guests and amused their eleven children. Even more satisfying is the Great Chamber above it, which contains a splendid Elizabethan bed from Battle Abbey in Sussex and is roofed by a double-frame of oak beams as clean, strong and simple as the structure of a ship's hull. There are more splendid rooms in other houses of this date, but there is none so satisfying and none which makes more immediate an impression of what it felt like to be caged in oak, bedded in oak and surrounded by oak furniture that was passed devotedly from father to son.

After seeing these two main rooms of Lawrence Washington's house, one could expect the Queen Anne wing to be out of harmony with the memory of the family whose name is invariably linked with Sulgrave. If only the Hodges family had inhabited it, the manor might not now even exist. In fact John Hodges' north wing is in itself a period-piece of great charm, by which he contrived, consciously or not, to extend the Elizabethan building in the style of his own age without destroying the unity of the house. The Queen Anne addition is only slightly more stylish than the better type of contemporary farm-house, and the kitchen, now splendescent with the copper and polished steel of an early eighteenth-century range imported from Hampshire, was the main room of the later part of the house.

Sulgrave lies on the outskirts of its manorial village, surrounded by the cornfields and sheep-walks out of which the village grew and by which it still lives. Before the days of the railway and bus it was so isolated that it and three neighbouring hamlets were known as 'the lost villages'. Now it is known to most Englishmen and many Americans as the place where the Washingtons settled and from which they carried to America the greatest name in its history. But would Sulgrave be a place of pilgrimage instead of Washington in County Durham, were it not for the manor-house, so faithfully restored by the two nations, which so well preserves the spirit of Christian neighbourliness with which the Washington family were endowed?

Montacute
Somerset

IT IS FORTUNATE THAT ONE OF THE VERY FIRST HOUSES to survive from the late Elizabethan period should also be one of the least altered. Changes were made to Montacute, notably to the west front towards the end of the eighteenth century and to the interior by Lord Curzon at the beginning of the twentieth, but they were made with taste and tact. Its convenience was thereby improved, but its Elizabethan character has remained unaffected. What we see today is substantially the house which Sir Edward Phelips, a Somerset landowner and lawyer who rose to be Speaker of the House of Commons and Master of the Rolls, began to build in the last decade of the sixteenth century. The date 1601, carved above the east doorway, probably marks the year of its completion.

Sir Edward collaborated with a local master-mason of near-genius named William Arnold. The latter was a little less than the 'architect' of Montacute, in the sense that we would employ the term today, for the difference in social standing between himself and his employer, and the energy with which a great man of the times applied himself to the building of a house designed to display and heighten his status, would have made such a relationship impossible. But Arnold was also much more than clerk-of-works. Probably he had a freer hand than Lyminge had at Hatfield, or than Arnold himself was given by Robert Cecil, first Earl of Salisbury, at Cranborne a few years later. There is no question that his influence at Montacute was dominant, and that the chief credit for this remarkable house belongs to him.

The Arnold-Phelips, or Phelips-Arnold, conception of domestic grandeur is best illustrated by the east front, originally the entrance front. From this direction the house at first appears rather flat – three superimposed tiers of enormous mullioned windows extending across a façade nearly two hundred feet in width and ninety feet high. But if it were nothing more than a succession of grids let in to a stone cliff, Montacute would be a disappointment; and the first sight of Montacute never disappoints. The front, though perfectly symmetrical, is full of vitality. The changes in the building-line occur effortlessly, sometimes by simple projections, as in the porch and wings, sometimes by subtle curvature, as in the accentuated lines of the Flemish-type gables, sometimes by a line deliberately angled, as in the shallow bay-windows at the ends of the wings.

*An aerial photograph taken from the
north-west. The porch in the centre of this front
is earlier than the house, and was brought to
Montacute from Clifton Maybank in 1787,
when the entrance was switched to this side.*

The east front is abundantly decorated, but one has to search for the decorative elements that the eye has unconsciously taken in. At ground level there are six steps down from the terrace to the gravel path, not meanly centred on the porch, but spread across the full width between the wings. On the terrace itself are six free-standing columns, matching the columnar structure of the chimneys high above. There are curved cornices to some of the windows, niches with scalloped canopies, curious circular indentations in the walls like impressions left by cannon balls which failed to penetrate, but probably intended for terracotta medallions; there are three classical entablatures marking the ceiling-levels within, the centre one plain, the uppermost enlivened by stone dentils and the bottom one by a primitive triglyph frieze. There is a handsome cornice and a balustrade with obelisks at roof-level, and below it, between the windows of the top storey, the most daring and pleasing device of all – the statues of the Nine Worthies (Joshua, David, Judas Maccabeus, Hector, Alexander, Julius Caesar, Arthur, Charlemagne and Godfrey of Bouillon), all dressed as Roman soldiers and gesturing with apparent unconcern in the security of their lofty niches. One reason why this amount of detail, much of it Italian in inspiration, is not only acceptable in a very English house but passes almost unnoticed by a superficial glance, is that every part of it, even the row of statues, is made of the same stone. Montacute is built of stone from the local quarry of Ham Hill, which has greatly enriched southern Somerset and the adjacent parts of Dorset. It is a tawny ochre stone which absorbs rather than reflects the sun, and is particularly attractive to lichens which give it a mottled appearance and spread the colour unevenly as if on a painter's palette. It exudes colour like honey, in much the same way as long-weathered Pentelic marble. Equally effective is the use of the same stone inside the house, where it appears creamier, richer and skin-smooth in texture. But the outer walls of Montacute in a setting sun are of such loveliness that if it were the face of a quarry instead of the face of a house, one's pleasure at the sight of it would scarcely be diminished.

Below the east front extends a forecourt. The centre of it is grassed, and it is closed on three sides by a balustrade exactly matching that on the roof, raised above the flower-beds on low walls. Along the top are spaced slender obelisks, with stone lanterns at the central points and identical domed pavilions at each end where the garden is divided from the park. These pavilions are Arnold's masterpiece. Nobody having once seen them could ever again say that Elizabethan builders were incapable of delicacy. They are, and apparently always have been, quite empty, without even an internal floor to divide them into the two storeys which the windows suggest from outside. They are follies, architectural dolls' houses, Elizabethan editions, as Avray Tipping first suggested, of the towers flanking a fortified mediaeval forecourt. On each of them, the ogee roof curves upwards with the grace of a swan's neck to a pinnacle topped by a sort of stone astrolabe. The oriel windows swing outwards from all four sides with a certainty of line and proportion that is amazing in something so miniature. On arriving, on leaving, and throughout a prolonged visit to Montacute, one's eye wanders back to them again and again.

The other side of the house, the west side, has been the entrance front since the late eighteenth century. In 1786–7, Edward Phelips, who inherited Montacute at the age of nine and lived there for sixty-three years, did away with the old frontal approach, removed a lake from the park and the bridge which crossed it (both can be seen in the Collinson drawing, made in the year of the change) and seems to have re-used the balustrade of the latter to construct the low wall which closes the forecourt between the two pavilions. But he did much more than this. He bought the porch and other ornamental features of a late-Tudor house six miles away in Dorset called Clifton Maybank, and fitted them boldly between the two wings of the west front of Montacute. The Clifton Maybank façade formed the centre of the new entrance front, and although it was some fifty years earlier in date, it was made of the same Ham Hill stone and anticipated the Renaissance detail of Montacute so brilliantly that it would be difficult for anybody but an expert to tell them apart. Indeed, the reliefs and finials around and over the porch are among the most vigorous and pleasing work to be seen here. It was a splendid adaptation, and incidentally a noble feat of rescue work, for Clifton Maybank was then being pulled down and these parts of its structure were acquired at the sale of the materials. But it also served a functional purpose. It supplied the first and second storeys of Montacute with internal corridors, which added greatly to the convenience of a house where even a bedroom could only be entered by passing through another.

To the north and south there are ornamental gardens, which form, together with the forecourt, three large panels of green from which the ochre house stands up magnificently. The only flower-borders are those down each side of the forecourt, planted from designs made by V. Sackville-West in the 1950s. The other two gardens rely for their effect on large lawns, gravel walks, sentinel rows of clipped yews and a serpentine balustrade around a central pond. The north garden follows in essentials the Elizabethan plan. It is confined by paths raised on broad parapets around the whole circuit of the lawn and with a vista at the far end over the Somerset countryside. From this point, too, one can see the north front of the house to perfection. This façade is plain compared to the main fronts, but is relieved by the great oriel window of the Long Gallery, its corbels supporting the light framework of the window with the strength and flexibility of an elephant's trunk.

The interior of the house remains almost unaltered from the day it was built. Montacute is therefore the *locus classicus* in which to study the transition from a Tudor clumsiness of plan to an arrangement of rooms which falls little short of modern conceptions of convenience. Of course, there are deficiencies. The original absence of corridors has already been mentioned, and the distance between the kitchens in the south wing and the family's main dining-room on the first floor of the north wing involved a walk – or rather a procession of dish-bearing footmen – of over seventy yards. All the rooms are large and very light. The huge windows not only enliven the exterior by their patterns of mullions and transoms and diamond panes catching the light from slightly different angles, but turn the rooms into boxes as airy as bird-cages.

One of the two Elizabethan pavilions which flank the original forecourt. They were purely decorative, and have never contained a floor separating the two storeys.

OPPOSITE ABOVE *The library,
formerly the Great Chamber. The
panelling and heraldic glass are
original to the house.*

OPPOSITE BELOW *The Great Hall,
looking towards the stone screen. The
curious Ionic columns betray the
uncertainty with which William Arnold
handled classical themes, contrasting with
his sure treatment of traditional English
motifs.*

*The north staircase, which runs in broad
flights of stone steps from the hall to the
Great Chamber round a central pier of
solid masonry.*

The finest of them is the library, previously the dining-room and before that the Great Chamber where the Phelips may have held their manorial courts. It has four windows, two of them of twelve lights, one of eighteen and the fourth of twenty-one. The upper two rows of lights are in each case filled with armorial bearings of coloured glass. An inner porch of richly carved wood leads into the room, and the chimneypiece of Portland stone, the panelling and plasterwork frieze are all original. The bookshelves are nineteenth-century, but excellent of their kind.

If no other room quite approaches the Great Chamber in restrained magnificence, the whole interior of Montacute repays the most careful study. In every part of the house one finds evidence of Arnold's skill. He was happier when improvising on the traditional English forms than when adapting half-understood Continental models, and much of the interior work of the latter type contrasts crudely and unexpectedly with his use of classical motifs on the façades. An instance is to be found in the hall, where the screen, apart from its two lovely arches, is a fantastic jumble of styles and different coloured stone, while the plaster panel filling the upper part of the opposite wall is a spontaneous expression of native humour. In other places, Arnold relied on the simplest grouping of his excellent materials. The north staircase could not be plainer in its construction, with great blocks of Ham Hill stone forming the short flights of steps, punctuated by quarter and half-landings, and a massive core of the same stone. In its own way, it is more successful than the open timber staircases which were to become fashionable only a few years later in great houses like Knole and Hatfield.

In recent years the National Trust have restored the Long Gallery at the top of the house, a magnificent room a hundred and seventy-two feet long by twenty feet broad, with small chambers opening off it. It is hung with Tudor and Jacobean portraits on loan from the National Portrait Gallery.

The latest phase in the history of Montacute nearly ended in tragedy. The Phelips family, having failed during the eighteenth and nineteenth centuries to marry the necessary number of heiresses, could not afford to maintain so large a house. They let it to various tenants, including Lord Curzon, who lived there on and off between 1915 and his death in 1925. But soon afterwards the Phelips reluctantly decided to sell Montacute. A house which had cost £20,000 to build in 1600 was bought in 1931 for £30,000 by a great benefactor of English architecture, Mr E. E. Cook, and presented by him to the Society for the Protection of Ancient Buildings, which in turn handed it over to the National Trust. It does not give the impression of a museum. One of the reasons is that there are no mats or guard-ropes to spoil the interior: another, that the house has drunk in the affection of all who care for it or visit it, just as it drinks in the sunlight through its great windows and lovely stone.

Castle Fraser
Aberdeenshire

THE BEST MOMENT TO SEE CASTLE FRASER for the first time is in the evening of a summer's day. You catch sight of it across an open park of a verdant trimness which one associates more with England than Scotland, half-hidden by the trees but gleaming palely between them, its major towers repeating the rotundity of their trunks and its upperworks their crowns. The house lies low in a shallow valley, rising from grass and gravel, with nothing, not even a garden, to distract the eye from its original period and lines. Sharp it is, with its poignard turret-tops, but its rounded towers swell like lighthouses, and it stands firmly self-contained, a mixture of architectural sexes, masculine as far as the roof-line, feminine above, a page torn from an illuminated Book of Hours. It is stubbornly defensive, yet contains no hint of menace. A secret place; a haunted place. Its walls, where exposed, are as rough as stone just taken from the moor, but careful craftsmanship is evident in the survival of even its most delicate parts.

A castle? Yes, in more than name, for it was built to resist intrusion if not attack, and many of its features are derived from the keeps of mediaeval Scotland. But it is a house, too, since as the towers mount upwards they bifurcate into turrets and dormer windows, promising comfort and seclusion within, and on the north side two companionable wings enclose a courtyard by which the visitor feels welcomed and drawn in. To this unique product of Scottish architecture the name 'tower-house' is usually given. It is a good one, since it suggests both the history of this type of building and the combination of austerity and high spirits which were characteristic of the age. We call it romantic, because its turrets, its apparent lack of symmetry, its hard thick walls and the surprise of coming upon something so Gothic in the middle of radiant countryside make it seem far older than it is, representative of an age and attitudes as remote from our own as the true castles of the robber-barons of the Western Isles. We expect, half-hope, to find it a ruin. When we discover it to be intact, in part inhabited and wholly inhabitable, we are anxious to discover why men chose to build like this only three-and-a-half centuries ago, and to analyse its weird perfection.

Nobody could deny the builders of Castle Fraser a sense of proportion. When you consider how the arrangement and decoration of a normal house

79

have here been reversed, with the most glorious effects reserved for the upper storeys, it is surprising that it does not seem top-heavy or absurd. How has this balance been achieved? By much the same methods as a man-of-war. The poops, masts and gun-turrets spring from its upperworks, while the carcass is strong and slim. Although there is immense variety in its silhouette (therefore it can be viewed from every direction with equal pleasure), the scale of its vertical projections is in perfect harmony with the mass of its supporting towers. The skyline of an ordinary house is usually a cluster of chimneys which the eye accepts as a domestic necessity, as one day, by force of habit, it may come to accept a thicket of television aerials. But at Castle Fraser the chimneys are quite unobtrusive, and we have in their place tall conical or ogival caps rising to about the same height as chimneys, but by their shape, size and disposition infinitely more satisfying and suggestive. Horizontally as well as vertically the façades of the house combine solidity with surprise. There are frequent re-entrants where one tower joins another at right-angles or on a curve; a strong belt of carved stone at two-thirds of the height, as pronounced as the embroidered neckline to a shirt; a grouping of ringed corbels to support the turrets; and rows of windows disposed symmetrically to relieve, but not weaken, the massiveness of the keep. The colour of the walls is pinky-grey where they are 'harled' (covered with a weatherproof rendering of lime and sand), and rough in texture, like porridge, when they are not. Against them gently stir the shadows of the surrounding trees.

The temptation to seek a French influence in the architecture of Castle Fraser must be resisted. Certainly there was a strong cultural link between France and Scotland, and French masons are known to have worked on the royal palaces of this period. But the builders of the house, the Frasers of the late sixteenth and early seventeenth centuries, had no close connections with France, and its master-mason is known to have been a certain Bell, a member of a family of local craftsmen. Besides, only the turret-tops are superficially French. Where in France would you find squat roundels hanging like wasp-nests from the eaves, or such blankness of the lower walls, or the stepped string-course which wanders between and under the corbelling of the turrets? It is simpler to search for the origin of these tower-houses in Scotland itself, for in all parts of the country, in ruin or in perfect preservation, one can see examples of their antecedents, and follow the slow adaptation of ancient forms of fortification to the demand for greater comfort and convenience. Sometimes, as at Huntly Castle, also in Aberdeenshire, one can see all phases of construction and reconstruction, from the twelfth century to the seventeenth, in a single group. Internal partition-walls multiply; towers are thrown out from the main keep for defence and to provide private rooms leading off the hall; dormer-windows advance from behind the parapet flush with the outer walls; battlements become balustrades and wall-top defences ornamental turrets. All these developments are well documented in stone. Castle Fraser is the direct descendant of the thirteenth-century keep.

The central keep, with its added towers, dates substantially from 1550. The two long wings, of which one is here visible, were added in 1656.

What is surprising is that the Scottish nobility of the period immediately following the union of the two Crowns did not abandon their ancestral tradition more completely. After all, they were not untravelled ignoramuses. They had in the palaces of Stirling, Linlithgow, Holyrood House and Falkland superb examples of the new 'horizontal' style of building, which did not require the ladies of the house always to be ascending and descending tight spiral staircases between sweating walls, nor the laird to dine in the same hall where his henchmen slept. Their fidelity to the tower-house is ascribed to sentiment, to the shortage of brick and timber (the roof-beams for the wings at Castle Fraser had to be imported from Norway), to the desire to impress by sheer height, and to the needs of defence. This last explanation is not wholly convincing. Although the walls were six to nine feet thick at the base and pitted with holes for muskets, the tower-house was utterly defenceless against artillery, and there were no protective outworks, not even a moat or a ditch. Its situation cannot have been chosen by anyone who wished to keep the surrounding country under constant watch. The lower walls are bare, but not windowless. Those in the round tower extend almost to the ground, and the four great windows of the hall on the first floor appear to be original, though they may have been enlarged. Fraser does not have the closed look of a castle, but the frank look of a house.

One additional reason why Castle Fraser was built like this, as one of the last and certainly one of the greatest of the tower-houses, is that its roots may already have been there. Archaeologists are still disputing whether the building incorporates work earlier than the mid-sixteenth century, but the most authoritative of them, Dr W. Douglas Simpson, thinks that it does not. What is certain is that the square tower known as Michael Tower, after its builder Michael Fraser, cannot be later than 1576, for a carved stone bears that date, and it may have been erected even earlier as a hunting-lodge. The main block and the circular tower, diagonally opposite Michael Tower, were added in about 1600 in the same general style, following the tradition that you enlarged your house by adding towers. Then, some fifteen years later, the whole building was heightened and transformed by Michael's son, Andrew, who retained the lower structure as far as the fretted band and added above it the whole complicated panoply of turrets, dormers and the steeply pitched roof. The dormers bear the date of completion, 1618. The wings were added, also by Andrew, in 1621–36. Thus the minimum period of building extends over sixty years, and during that time the tastes and habits of the lairds had changed considerably. The lower and older parts of the castle are still mediaeval in spirit; the upper parts and wings reflect the greater stability of the times, and the influence, though much diluted, of the Renaissance. The Frasers telescoped into sixty years what English architects had taken three hundred to evolve, because the English started earlier. But it should be remembered that Castle Fraser is contemporary with such English houses as Knole and Blickling, and even (in its last and most dramatic phase) with Inigo Jones's Wilton. There was still a very wide gap.

The interior reveals better than the outside the sixteenth-century Frasers' reluctance to break with the past. The room at the base of the round tower is dungeon-like in its dim rotundity, though it was probably never used for

The turret-tops could be mistaken for French, but the influence is that of mediaeval Scottish castles. They look splendid from a distance, and form interesting annexes to the rooms inside.

The roofs of the wings from one of the higher towers. These 17th-century wings formed a service courtyard at the back of the castle.

anything but storage, while the kitchens on the ground floor are more like cellars than rooms, mere cavities in the vast foundations, but whitened and well-lit, with walls, ceilings and fireplaces bowed with the strain of supporting so great a bulk. On the floor above is the main suite – the hall, and a withdrawing room in each tower. The ceilings are barrel-vaulted. There is a monastic severity about the hall, from the huge fireplace at one end to the stone window-seat at the other. The granite expressed and imposed a Spartan way of life. Of course, it was not necessarily always as gaunt as it appears today. One must in imagination add the colours of tapestry, silver, heraldic shields and jewelled clothes. In the near-contemporary Aberdeenshire tower-houses of Crathes, Midmar and Craigievar one can still see panelling, wall-painting and plasterwork of which Castle Fraser must surely once have had its share. But its interior can never have been as splendid as theirs, for later owners would have been at pains to preserve whatever seventeenth-century decorations they found, as they so faithfully preserved the outside. There are other features of Castle Fraser which slightly chill the blood. A chamber concealed in the groin of the hall's vaulting, and approachable only through a trapdoor in the laird's bedroom above, enabled him to overhear every word spoken in the window-seat of the hall. There is a similar eaves-dropping chamber at Speke Hall in Lancashire, but it dates from a hundred years earlier. Again the Scottish time-lag in morals and manners! In all parts of the house one finds spy-holes and gun-loops, traps for the treacherous and unwary, and, not surprisingly, a ghost, bloodstained steps and inexplicable sounds after dark.

The last of the male Frasers of that line, Charles Fraser the Younger of Castle Fraser, was killed in 1746, fighting for the Young Pretender at Culloden, and the property passed to his maiden sister, Elysa Fraser, who held it until 1814. She made various improvements to the house, including a new front door on the south front, not ill-suited to its old walls, and a timber staircase, since removed, to supplement the spiral stairs which still make access to the upper floors so perplexing to a stranger. It was she, and her immediate successors, who partitioned and redecorated the loftier part of the house, and so radically altered its arrangements that it is now almost impossible to recover the seventeenth-century plan. Their improvements made the house habitable without disturbing its elevations, which remain Castle Fraser's chief glory. But except for flats in the two wings, it is now unoccupied.

The main room of Castle Fraser, which well illustrates the reluctance of the Fraser family to break with the past. 'The granite expressed and imposed a Spartan way of life.'

Hardwick Hall
Derbyshire

HARDWICK IS ECCENTRIC, WEIRD AND UNCOMFORTABLE. But it also happens to be one of the most beautiful buildings ever created. Nobody who has ever wandered round its rooms and gardens can ever again be in doubt what he is by nature. If the house appeals to you through and through, if you find yourself lowering your voice in instinctive response to the quietness of the rooms, if you enjoy the feel of rush matting and stone steps beneath your feet, if the crookedness of a door does not irritate you and you have no desire to paper an expanse of whitewashed wall, then Hardwick is for you: you are an incurable romantic.

It is probably the finest surviving house of the late Elizabethan period. One does not associate that quarrelsome age with muted tones or an attitude of reserve, and even less its builder, Elizabeth Shrewsbury, known throughout history as 'Bess of Hardwick'. But here she managed to balance overstatement outside by understatement inside. The exterior of the house is splendidly arrogant and adventurous; the interior is as cool and sedate as a convent. It seems almost impossible that those windows, despite their huge size, should let in so little glare.

The story of Bess of Hardwick must be briefly retold, for the romance of the place is inextricably bound up with it. She was born in the old manor-house at Hardwick in 1520, the third daughter of a country squire of little importance and less wealth. The house, which stood within a stone's throw of the present Hardwick, was a three-storey, stone-gabled building, little more than a farm-house. At the age of twelve Elizabeth was married to a near-neighbour's son, Master Robert Barlow, aged fourteen, who died a few months after the wedding, leaving considerable property to his young widow. She was twenty-seven when she married her second husband, Sir William Cavendish from Suffolk, who held an important position at Court and made a fortune from it. Sir William, dying in 1557, left her all his possessions, despite the claims of his children by two former wives. Three years afterwards she hooked Sir William St Loe, Captain of the Queen's Guard and Grand Butler of England. The sequel can by this time be foreseen: Sir William died four or five years later, and once again Bess netted much of his property. Finally, in 1568, she found a fourth and even richer and more distinguished husband, the sixth Earl of

The initials ES, *for Elizabeth Shrewsbury, stand fretted against the skyline of her magnificent house.*

Shrewsbury. A condition of their marriage, imposed by Bess, was that two of her Cavendish children should marry two of the Earl's children soon after she married the father. Lord Shrewsbury had seven houses of his own (Sheffield Castle, Sheffield Manor, Worksop Manor, Buxton Hall, Rufford Abbey, South Wingfield Manor and Shrewsbury House in London), and Bess at least four. By then she was the richest and most formidable woman in England, with one exception: the Queen. No mean achievement for the third daughter of an insignificant squire.

The strangest part of this extraordinary story was still to come. Lord Shrewsbury was appointed jailer to Mary Queen of Scots, if by that term one can understand a man of great courtesy, undeniably susceptible to his prisoner's charms, who entertained her for fifteen years in the protective custody of his many mansions. Bess became acutely jealous of her, and for the last few years of his life she was not on speaking terms with her husband. However, she was quite well enough off to indulge still further her passion for building. She rebuilt her ancestral home at Hardwick to such vast dimensions that her father's little hall was quite lost within it. No sooner was Lord Shrewsbury in his grave – for even she had not quite the face to do it during his lifetime – than she began at the age of seventy to construct her last and greatest house. This was Hardwick Hall, not a hundred yards away from the 'old' hall which she continued to enlarge simultaneously with the erection of the 'new' hall, striding imperiously between the workmen from one to the other. The two buildings stand virtually side by side, the old hall now a ruin, the new hall a lasting memorial to her energy and taste.

Elizabeth Shrewsbury signed the house with her initials in fretted stone against the skyline. She had every claim to do so, for not only was she its begetter, but the full building accounts which have happily survived, show that she checked every detail of expenditure and supervised every phase of the work. Possibly Robert Smythson, who had played a big part in the design of Longleat and Wollaton, gave her professional help, but it is difficult to withhold from Bess herself the credit for the novelty and swagger of Hardwick. The whole building bears the impress of her character. She was a taskmistress who would stand no incompetence from others, but allowed herself the privilege of frequent changes of mind. Thus an item in the accounts would be crossed out, and against it, in the Countess' bold hand, is written, 'pott out by me'; or, 'because the walls ryse and be not well nor all of one colore, the most [they must] be wheyted [whitened] at the plasterers charge'. On another occasion she ordered that the turret-windows be heightened by an extra row of lights after they had been finished. One can imagine her standing between her buildings and deciding that there was still more wall than glass, and that the proportions must be reversed, whatever the expense.

In October 1593, only two-and-a-half years after the foundations were laid, the core of the house was finished. From the garden forecourt the west front rises tier upon tier of sparkling glass, the windows increasing in magnificence, like her marriages, as they mount upwards. There is not much surface decoration. The Tuscan colonnade between the two wings and the roof

ABOVE *The portrait of Bess of Hardwick still hangs against the tapestry of the Long Gallery where she placed it.*

OPPOSITE *The Long Gallery at Hardwick. It is the second longest gallery in Britain (after Montacute's), and runs the whole length of the east front. The gallery was designed to fit the tapestries which Bess acquired from Belgium shortly before she built the house.*

OVERLEAF LEFT *The east front of Montacute, originally the entrance front. It has remained virtually unaltered since its completion in 1601. Between the windows of the top storey stand statues of the Nine Worthies.*

OVERLEAF RIGHT *The room at the foot of Castle Fraser's round tower. These lower rooms 'are more like cellars than rooms, mere cavities in the vast foundations, but whitened and well-lit, with ceilings bowed with the strain of supporting so great a bulk.'*

balustrade above it are the only external concessions to classical fashion. The windows need no borders to enhance the splendour of their glass, the mullions and transoms forming ladders between the rows of diamond panes. It is basically a three-storey building, but without the turrets it would be little more than a smaller Longleat. The turrets were the master-stroke. They are purely decorative: five of them can only be approached from the leads of the roof, with a staircase in the sixth. One feels nothing but sympathy for the men-servants who were forced to sleep in them as late as the nineteenth century, but they not only give Hardwick its romantic skyline, which seems from a distance more like a castle than a house, but break up the four façades with bays and recesses making the whole building glitter.

There are three particular architectural features within the house which no visitor should miss: the staircase, the High Great Chamber and the Gallery. The staircase is built of stone. It has no mouldings, no carpet and the mere pretence of a banister. It is exceptionally wide, and owing to the slight movement of its structure, part of it tilts at odd angles. It does not mount within a continuous rectangular stair-well, but wanders lengthwise through the house like a passage. At intervals the broad straight steps turn into spirals where shortage of space demanded it, radiating from the newel like the ribs of a fan. The most beautiful effects of line and shadow are thereby achieved. It is hard to say whether Bess continued them deliberately or not. They look accidental, but it is difficult to say to what extent her eye for dramatic effect could reach.

But the High Chamber is no accident. Sacheverell Sitwell has called it 'the most beautiful room, not in England alone, but in the whole of Europe'. It is extremely difficult to illustrate this claim photographically, for the faded potpourri of the tapestries and moulded frieze merge into a monochrome blur, and the effect of the room depends upon seeing it in all its subtle colouring and dimensions. The proportions are extremely simple, a rectangular box extended on one side by a window embrasure, itself as big as a normal parlour, which occupies the whole space within one of the turrets. The immensely tall windows of the third storey throw diamond patterns across the rush-matted floor. The ceiling is quite plain, without even the simplest cornice. The walls are hung with eight Brussels tapestries purchased by Bess in 1587, in time to design the room to contain them exactly. Above them runs a plaster frieze of Diana and her hunters, sometimes as crude in detail as cave-paintings, but wonderfully beautiful in their overall effect. They illustrate to perfection a particular quality of Hardwick, that while it owes much of its inspiration to classical sources, the execution is entirely English. Among the 375 names of workmen recorded in the accounts, there is scarcely one recognizable as foreign.

The Gallery opens off the High Great Chamber. Here the dominant colour is the lavender of the tapestries, woven in Flanders in 1578 and bought by Bess in 1592. Once again they determined the dimensions of the room. It runs the length of the east front and is lit by twenty of the tallest windows. Its immense length, second only to the gallery at Montacute and of infinitely greater

*The house is basically a rectangular
block of three storeys, to which Bess,
with a stroke of genius, added six towers
rising above the roof-line.*

subtlety, turns the far end into a pool of hazy colour. Standing in this
stupendous room one feels overwhelmed, not by the size of it, but by the
creative energy of the woman who devoted the last years of her life to realizing
the dream of her old age. The portrait of Bess of Hardwick hangs against the
gallery tapestries, surrounded by three of the four husbands whose wealth she
ransacked to such glorious effect.

*The High Great Chamber, which
Sacheverell Sitwell has called 'the most
beautiful room, not in England alone,
but in the whole of Europe'.*

Knole
Kent

'I, WHO AM A LOVER OF ALL ANTIQUITIES,' wrote Edmund Burke to John Frederick Sackville, third Duke of Dorset, 'must be a very great admirer of Knole. I think it is the most interesting thing in England.' That was two hundred years ago. What then must it mean to us, who can see the same buildings, decoration and contents which Burke saw, virtually unchanged since his time? Set us down there a further century back, in 1670: still no change. A further century, in 1570; then one would see considerable differences in the interior, but few outside. In 1470: then the greater part of the house was being built. Five centuries of continuous occupation is no great rarity among English houses, but if the last three-and-a-half have left almost no mark upon the house, it becomes something remarkable. If, further, it happens to be one of the largest houses in the country – containing 365 rooms, it is said, but nobody has ever counted them – and has belonged to a noble family who were wealthy at a time when wealth was used to greatest advantage, it becomes a phenomenon. Choose your century, from the fifteenth to the seventeenth, and you can find corners or whole suites of rooms at Knole which will evoke its atmosphere exactly. Ask to see the eighteenth, and you will be shown only the clock-tower, a few pieces of furniture and a single fireplace. The nineteenth? A row of windows in the orangery on the garden front. The twentieth? You left it outside.

This does not mean that Knole is an uninhabitable museum, for a condensation of its history must disregard the constant process of repair and modernization which today enables nearly forty people to make the house their home and its care their main concern. Nor does it mean that because Knole is old it must be melancholy. V. Sackville-West, who was born there and wrote its history, said that Knole 'has the deep inward gaiety of some very old woman who has always been beautiful, who has had many lovers and seen many generations come and go, smiled wisely over their sorrows and their joys and learnt an imperishable secret of tolerance and humour'. To endow a house with human perceptions of this kind is a romantic way of saying that those who built it, enlarged it, furnished it and embellished it did so in the hope that later generations would approve their motives and share their tastes, and that their hopes were not disappointed. A house, being more

*The south and east fronts of the house from a corner of
the garden. The tall windows in the right-centre are those
of the chapel, and to the right of them is the row of
gables added by Thomas Sackville to the fifteenth-century
building.*

*Inside the Green Court, the first and largest of the seven
courts round which the house is built. The clock-tower
was one of the few later additions to the main
fifteenth-century structure.*

durable than its owners, is a record of their passage. Stone, brick and timber cannot smile on them: but they have smiled on it. In time their affection for it becomes, by legitimate analogy, its affection for them.

Certainly Knole is a very agreeable place to live in. It has a collegiate layout, court leading into court through arches in the cross-wings, and it increases in intimacy as the womb of the house is reached. The courts both divide and link. They break up the great grey mass into detached units, so that the house has very many external façades, each different, each a surprise: but at the same time they are courts to cross, treading on grass or gravel or paving-stones or cobbles, and courts to look into from upstairs windows, secluded and differently shadowed, but remaining part of the house although open to the sky. There are seven of them in all. Two are little more than light-wells; one is an open, irregular passageway from the kitchen to the hall; but the other two, the Green Court and the Stone Court, are noble in proportions and form the main entrance, one behind the other, giving Knole its chief architectural distinction. From inside, the house does not appear so very large, or it may be that familiarity reduces its scale, since one comes to take for granted the distances to be covered in passing from one corner to another, and much of the house consists in outbuildings or 'showrooms' where one only penetrates for special purposes. But from outside, particularly the north-east, where the park rises to one of the loveliest cricket-grounds in England, you look over a cataract of roofs and towers and the courts are lost between them, trebling the area covered by actual buildings. It resembles more a small town like Urbino or Vézelay than a house. Nor is it easy from this distance to disentangle the splendid parts from the merely functional, or one date of construction from another. The plainest stone-facing or gable-ends can conceal the finest rooms; the sturdiest battlements surmount a garage and a slaughter-house. All is built of the same material, Kentish ragstone capped by brown tiles, and the house seems to resist dissection into historical periods, for it is all very much of one character if not all of one piece. The attempt, however, must be made, and except for the very earliest period it is found to be surprisingly simple.

It is simple because Knole is really the creation of two men: Thomas Bourchier, Archbishop of Canterbury, between 1456 and 1486; and Thomas Sackville, first Earl of Dorset, between 1603 and 1608. Other Archbishops and other Dorsets completed or extended what they began, but they did so in the same style and with the same purpose, and their individual contributions were in a comparatively minor key. No-one knows for certain whether any part of an earlier mediaeval manor-house survives, nor indeed whether it ever existed. Knole was a manor in the thirteenth century, but a manor does not necessarily imply a manor-house, since its owners had other houses nearby, and on this site there could have been nothing but farm-buildings. On the north side, however, there is a jumble of towers, gables and entrances among which archaeologists may one day decipher early mediaeval work. If so, it was probably modest, for Bourchier paid no more than £266.1.4 for the whole manor in 1456. The written evidence is contradictory. Richard Kilburne, in

his *Survey of Kent*, published in 1659, says that 'there Bourchier built a faire house', which was enlarged by his successors in the See of Canterbury. But Philipott, whose history of the county was published in the same year, says that Bourchier 'added much of Pompe and Magnificence by a new Supplement or Superstructure *to the ancient Pile or Fabrick*'; and the Lambeth Palace accounts of 1467–8 refer to 'repairs' at Knole and to 'a new tower' and 'a new solar', which suggest that something fairly substantial was there before. The point is important, because if Bourchier built the whole house on a virtually virgin site, Knole would be by far the largest private house surviving from the fifteenth century; but if he merely added to 'an ancient Pile', his work, while certainly on a princely scale, becomes an adaptation and not a wholly original enterprise. Without entering into further detail, it can be said that Knole was for eighty years the palace of five successive Archbishops of Canterbury, from Bourchier to Cranmer, and that each of them, but particularly Bourchier, contributed to the building which we see today. It is likely that nothing of any size except the clock-tower was added to it at a later date.

Henry VIII acquired Knole from Cranmer in 1538, and for nearly twenty years it was a royal palace. Queen Elizabeth gave it to her cousin, Thomas Sackville, later her Lord Treasurer and first Earl of Dorset, but the gift was subject to a lease which did not expire till the year of the Queen's death in 1603, and it was only in the last five years of his life that Lord Dorset was able to call it truly his own. He used those five years to transform it.

Dorset's work fuses beautifully with the Archbishops', although the whole of the early English Renaissance lay in between. There is nothing at Knole that can be for certain identified as Elizabethan, for its royal period left no obvious mark. What we see is a Jacobean rendering of a Perpendicular shell. Dorset achieved this feat by adding at significant points ornamentations which gave the house a more elegant and symmetrical appearance and greatly increased its commodiousness. Externally, he left intact the tall double-arches of the windows and the crenellations of the walls and towers; but he imposed on them the swirling Dutch gables and the sentinel leopards of his family crest, a Tuscan colonnade at the inner side of the Stone Court and a row of friendly gables above the eastern state-rooms. Internally, he lowered the high Gothic roof of the hall by a plastered ceiling and replaced Bourchier's screen by a Jacobean screen of barbaric sumptuousness; he remodelled the interior wall-facings, ceilings and fireplaces in almost every part of the house; he built a beautiful timber staircase, set leopards on its newel posts and painted its walls in *grisaille*; and he employed foreign craftsmen to embellish his window-reveals and to add decorative devices in plaster, wood-carving or paint to almost every internal surface that would take them. In all this work one traces a consistent taste: a feeling for the excellence of the Archbishops' work, and, except for the hall screen, a delicacy of touch which conforms well with what is known of his non-belligerent, reserved character. It should be remembered that before he took to politics Thomas Sackville was a poet who occupies a respectable place in the history of English literature.

This double origin of Knole explains the puzzling appearance of the house

The Great Hall was built about 1460, but the oak panelling, the screen and the plasterwork ceiling were added by Thomas Sackville, first Earl of Dorset, in about 1603. Above the screen is the Minstrels Gallery, pierced by wooden lattices.

from outside. How can so severe a house contrive to look so charming? How can the entrance front apparently only one step removed from a castle, convey so hospitable a welcome? The answer lies in the addition of the gables and their leopard-finials, an embellishment that grows out of the earlier work without unbalancing it, a stroke of architectural inventiveness and tact which could not have been bettered. Within the Green Court one discerns exactly the same motive. Here there was not even a basic symmetry for Dorset to work upon: the flanking towers were not of equal width and Bourchier's gatehouse was not central. Dorset destroyed nothing, but he pulled the façade together by two more gables ingeniously placed to disguise the lack of symmetry, and one likes to imagine that he was also responsible for turfing the courtyard with its two great squares of grass. He added further gables to the centre of the south, or garden, front. It was a process of softening and rounding. He found an edifice and turned it into a house.

The long galleries must also have been of his making, since no gallery of this size is known earlier than that at Hampton Court, which dates from the reign of Henry VIII. In Bourchier's day these rooms would have been divided for the great retinue that surrounded an Archbishop into a warren of chambers, alternately large and small. As Dorset's internal reconstruction barely tampered with the main fabric, it is remarkable how easily the rooms run together, gallery to bedroom, bedroom to dressing-room, Great Chamber (now called the Ballroom) to staircase, staircase to Hall, when the original disposition of rooms must have been quite different and the Archbishop's ground-plan is beyond recovery in the ingenuity of its reconstruction. Most Jacobean houses have one gallery: Knole has five, if one counts, as one should, the huge Retainers' Galleries running along the top of the house. They are rooms of controlled magnificence, which until the middle of the eighteenth century were the main living-quarters of the Sackville family together with the set of less grandiose apartments on the ground floor of the garden front. The latter were the only ones which the family permitted themselves to touch: here you will find that isolated eighteenth-century fireplace in a drawing-room adjoining the library, and *grisaille* paintings of the same date in the Colonnade. But the state-rooms, which have been open to the public for at least two hundred years, were regarded as sacrosanct, and the very thought of William Kent or Robert Adam or Wyatt daring to add their own version of refinement is an impertinence.

The Sackvilles deliberately cultivated the antique. Their furniture was often as much as a century old when it was first installed. We find, for instance, that in the little rooms allotted to Lady Betty Germain between 1720 and 1750, the carpet is late sixteenth-century, the chairs are Charles II, the stools Queen Anne, and her four-poster bed is mid-seventeenth century, and nobody has touched a single object since she was there. The Brown Gallery and the Leicester Gallery contain early seventeenth-century furniture in their original coverings that have no equal in any other collection: many of them were brought there from Hampton Court and Whitehall by the sixth Earl of Dorset, who died in 1705.

The Cartoon Gallery, so called from the copies of Raphael's cartoons by Daniel Mytens brought to Knole in 1701. The fireplace is Jacobean.

A Gorgon's head from the Jacobean
screen in the Great Hall.

Knole is undoubtedly one of the half-dozen greatest houses in Britain, whatever criteria of greatness are adopted. It is very large; it has a distinguished history; its two main periods blend with remarkable sympathy; its contents are unique; it remains in the occupation of the Sackvilles. It is, above all, as V. Sackville-West said, a very English house. 'It has the tone of England,' she wrote. 'It melts into the green of the garden turf, into the tawnier green of the park beyond, into the blue of the pale English sky.... The brown-red of these roofs is the brown-red of the roofs of humble farms and pointed oast-houses, such as stain over a wide landscape of England the quilt-like pattern of the fields.' Those words were written by one who never pretended to a scholar's knowledge of the history of architecture but loved the house as she might love a grandmother, sensing that it once had a youth but finding in it something much more identifiable and appealing, the serenity of a fine old age.

Hatfield
House
Hertfordshire

ROBERT CECIL, FIRST EARL OF SALISBURY, the builder of Hatfield House, was the second of the three members of his family who have become chief ministers of the Crown. The first was his father, Lord Burghley; the third, the Marquess of Salisbury who was three times Prime Minister to Queen Victoria. Robert Cecil remains the most enigmatic figure of the three. Although he was forceful and occasionally ruthless in his public life, his great office rendered him aloof, even friendless. The tension at which he lived in the later years of Queen Elizabeth and the early part of the reign of James I, when he was the butt of intrigue and slander by less brilliant men, was increased by his physical disabilities. Not much more than five foot three inches in height, he was partly crippled by a curvature of the spine which aroused the ridicule even of his cousin, Sir Francis Bacon. More affectionately, Queen Elizabeth would call him her 'little elf', and James I 'my little beagle', 'my pigmy'.

Of the two largest houses which his father built, Burghley, from which he took his title, descended to the Earl of Essex, and Theobalds so entranced James I that he suggested to his chief minister that he should exchange it for the royal palace at Hatfield, a suggestion which Robert Cecil found difficult to refuse. The old palace at Hatfield, built by Bishop Morton of Ely towards the end of the fifteenth century, had been the home, at times virtually the prison, of Henry VIII's children. While seated under an oak tree in the park (which, wired and pitifully battered, is still shown to visitors), Princess Elizabeth received the news that her sister Mary was dead and that she was now Queen of England.

As soon as the exchange of Theobalds for Hatfield had been completed in 1607, Robert Cecil began to build a vast new house for himself, a hundred yards south-east of the old palace. He was in a sense his own architect, for not only did he define its main floor-plans and elevations, but the men whom he employed on the actual construction – a factotum named Thomas Wilson, the head surveyor Robert Lyminge, the master-mason Conn, and a host of joiners, plasterers, inlayers, carvers, glass-painters and gardeners from England, France, Italy and Flanders – were required to submit their designs for his approval. The house was completed in five years, 1607–11. It was an extraordinary achievement of planning and organization. The stone was brought from Caen, where a special quarry was opened by licence of the

French king; marble from Carrara; bricks from the old palace; timber from the estate. Even before the house was half-built, the terraces were laid out around it, and John Tradescant, the first of the great English botanists, was scouring the Continent for unusual trees and plants.

Those same five years were Cecil's busiest. As the ablest administrator of his age he was running the country almost single-handed, and simultaneously was building Salisbury House in London, making extensive alterations to Cranborne in Dorset and managing distant estates like St Michael's Mount in Cornwall. As one walks through the immensely elaborate house today fresh from studying the manuscript records of its building, one can conceive something of the anxious urgency with which the different elements, often prefabricated in widely separated workshops, were fitted together with shipwright's precision. Anyone who has had the satisfaction of building or adapting a far more modest house can imagine the solace which Robert Cecil must have derived from the knowledge that his house was growing in his absence, and that one day soon he would sleep there. But his health broke under the strain of office. He stayed no more than eight nights at Hatfield before it was barely habitable, and died at Marlborough on 24 May 1612 at the age of forty-nine. It was left to his son to add the finishing touches.

Like Blickling, another great Jacobean house of which Robert Lyminge was part-architect, Hatfield illustrates perfectly what a nobleman of the early seventeenth century conceived to be the essentials of a private house fit to receive his Sovereign. The approach to it must be impressive, but not forbidding; the plan must allow for great state receptions as well as for privacy; the interior must incorporate works of art built into the fabric as fireplaces, ceilings, doorways, panelling and staircases to compensate for the comparative sparseness of contemporary furnishing; the house must be lit by great windows and warmed by capacious fires; and from the windows there must be views of formal gardens abruptly separated from the surrounding park.

In carrying out his ideas, Robert Cecil was part traditionalist, part innovator. Nowhere is the contrast better shown than by the two main fronts. The north front presents a façade which differs little from the accepted style of the late sixteenth century, a cliff of warm brick ridged by shallow bays and recesses and broken by tall, wide windows symmetrically disposed. Its rather overpowering, sawn-off appearance today is partly due to the substitution in the nineteenth century of plate-glass for the original small leaded panes and the removal of the ogee-shaped domes to the angle turrets, just visible in Knyff's and other eighteenth-century views of the house. But the south front represents a quite different conception of grandeur. Here the projecting east and west wings form a forecourt of great dignity, varied but not muddled, to which the central 'Italian' arcade, the Flemish-type gables and the white timber tower behind add a note of such elegance that it has been attributed to Inigo Jones, an attribution that the heavy Jacobean porch makes highly unlikely.

The house is in the shape of the Greek letter *pi*, or flattened U, the wings forming the two uprights. Cecil followed the Elizabethan style to the extent that he placed a great hall in the centre of his house, a long gallery and three or

*The north front, now the entrance front. Originally the
two corner towers were topped by cupolas.*

four large chambers on the first storey, and a chapel at the side. But in the west wing, which he intended for himself, and in the east wing for his guests, he inserted many smaller rooms, sometimes two or three in the width of the wing, which foreshadow the arrangements which we still accept as inevitable and right. Thus Hatfield is really three houses: the two wings, and the central block. Already the Great Hall and the Long Gallery were becoming anachronisms, although Hatfield would lose much of its splendour and interest without them. The Marble Hall, as it is called today, is the Jacobean elaboration of the hub of a mediaeval and Tudor house, retaining all the old features of screen, minstrels' gallery, bay-window and a huge fireplace, but functionally it was neither a hall in the old sense nor a room in the new sense. The convenience of the Long Gallery as a place for gentle exercise in cold or wet weather and in which to display furniture and pictures was not to compensate much longer for its awkwardness as a room for conversation nor for proportions that appeared increasingly clumsy to fastidious eyes. The gallery at Hatfield is one hundred and eighty feet long by only twenty wide, and although its decoration is superb of its kind, it is basically a long wooden box unrelieved by window-bays and relying on the two splendid fireplaces to break the monotony of its great length. The illustration of the crowded reception for Queen Victoria in 1846 shows its unsuitability for even the grandest occasions.

The south front. The forecourt and the elegant Renaissance loggias contrast with the austerity of the entrance front.

OPPOSITE *The east window of the chapel at Hatfield, painted in 1609 with scenes from the Old Testament by English, French and Flemish glass-painters.*

OVERLEAF LEFT *Silver furniture and a mirror in the King's Bedroom at Knole. All are dated about 1680, and form the most famous set of silver furnishing in Britain.*

OVERLEAF RIGHT *The Great Staircase at Knole, built between 1604 and 1608. It was the first timber staircase in Britain to be designed as a main architectural feature. The newel post is surmounted by the Sackville leopard.*

Angelis Abrahamo fidelis promittit Genesis
Angelus Matrer Iehan promisit Luce i.

Moyses in flumine seruatur Exodi 2.6.
Christus in Praesepi nascitur Luce 2.7.

Iacobus ad Labanum ab Hano
Christus in Ægiptum ab Herode

Ionas in Ventre piscis Ion.i.17
Christus in Visceribus Terræ Mat.12.4

Agnum Paschalem Israelita commedunt Exo.12.26
Cænam domini Christus instituit Mat.26.26

Delilah samsonem Philistiis tradidit Iudi.16.19
Iudas Christum Pharisæis prodidit Lucæ.22.

David Goliam Superat i.Sam:

A reception for Queen Victoria held in the Long Gallery in 1846. The gallery runs the whole length of the first floor, and apart from the gilding of the ceiling has remained unchanged since the building of the house.

OPPOSITE *The Marble Hall at Hatfield. To the right of the fireplace is Nicholas Hilliard's portrait of Queen Elizabeth I. The floor and ceiling paintings are Victorian additions.*

Hatfield owes as much to its fitted woodwork, marble and painted glass as to the works of art that were added subsequently. The hall screens, the Grand Staircase, the east window of the chapel and the ubiquitous Jacobean fireplaces produce an effect of Mannerist splendour. Jacobean ornamentation can be crisp and even playful, but it can suddenly degenerate into grossness and vulgarity. Strapwork on the ceilings and below the stairs, and stern caryatids thrusting their torsoes outwards from the walls or from below a balcony, contrast oddly at Hatfield with the lovely panels in the gallery and the balustrade of the staircase. The latter is the showpiece of the house, and rightly so, for not only is it the second staircase (after Knole's) to be treated as an architectural feature in itself, but it climbs from the level of the Marble Hall to the King James Drawing Room in short wide flights of steps, surmounted by snarling lions and laughing boys, that make it as free and vigorous as the ascent to the poop of a galleon.

In later centuries Hatfield was cared for by successive Lords Salisbury with skill and devotion. The house suffered one major disaster: in 1835 the central part of the west wing was burnt to the ground, and with it perished the aged Lady Salisbury, whose charming portrait as a young woman by Sir Joshua Reynolds makes so dreadful a death even harder to contemplate. Her son rebuilt the gaping hole, and glassed in the open loggia of the south front to form the Armoury, one of the most effective nineteenth-century

The Grand Staircase. The elaborately carved woodwork shows the influence of the Italian Renaissance on English ornament.

transformations to be seen in Britain. His son, the third Marquess, Queen Victoria's Prime Minister, renewed every part of the house that showed the defects of its age. Something of the many-sided character of the family is revealed in Lord David Cecil's casual account of the way in which the Prime Minister, a scientist as well as statesman, installed electricity at Hatfield in 1881: 'It was one of the first houses to be so lighted. The installation was very dangerous. Apart from the risks of shocks, the naked wires on the Gallery ceiling were apt to break into flame. The family sitting beneath nonchalantly threw up cushions to put the fire out and then went on with their conversation.'

Blickling
Hall
Norfolk

TO BEGIN A DESCRIPTION OF BLICKLING in a corner of its garden from which the house is not even visible may be thought eccentric. The first sight of the entrance front from the public road is so famous and breathtaking that every passing motorist halts instinctively to have a longer look. But the secret of the place is only discovered late in the day among the trees and flowering shrubs that stretch upwards from the east side of the house. Never has there been a garden quite like it, not at least since the eighteenth century, which created the idea of long avenues crossing each other at bosky *rond-points* and culminating in a white pavilion.

Memories of Versailles, Knyff's famous series of views and the legacies of Brown and Repton have prejudiced the English against the idea of the formal avenue. But an avenue is formal only if it is undeveloped or kept too trim. The garden at Blickling is neither. It remains decade after decade – and this is no paradox – at its prime. Elsewhere it might be called a wilderness, but here the term is quite inapt for something so leafy, so sunlit, so well-ordered and fulfilling so perfectly the intention which its creators never lived to see. Great arches of beech and oak form choirs and aisles, and under them grow azaleas, rhododendron, magnolias and the wild bluebell. At the end of each avenue is a stone urn or a glimpse from different angles of a Tuscan temple perfectly sited for the presiding deity of this glorious profusion, but more likely to have been used in the eighteenth century for tea-parties. Beyond stretches the park. At first the trees seem to continue the idea of the garden outside its encircling ha-ha, but then they thin out: grazing animals take the place of shrubs, and the silver crescent of a lake curves out of sight behind a natural hill.

That the eighteenth century should so strongly permeate the surroundings of a Jacobean house is not accidental. Much of its interior was refashioned at that time and the house recovered its former glory as a centre of arts and politics, as it did again in our own century when Lord Lothian was the owner. When Blickling was built, between 1616 and 1625, the arrangement and interior decoration of the rooms achieved standards of convenience and elegance which did not put later and more fastidious generations to discomfort or shame. It is true that they rebuilt one-and-a-half wings, but the one was reconstructed in 1769 because it was falling down, while the half was rebuilt by the second Earl of Buckinghamshire a few years later, with the apparent purpose of making room to hang a large and very beautiful tapestry which he had acquired as Ambassador to Catherine the Great. But when they rebuilt, they scarcely altered the original appearance of the house, using the same brick, respecting the old proportions and retaining the south and east fronts exactly as Robert Lyminge had erected them a century-and-a-half before.

Lyminge had been chief surveyor during the building of Hatfield, which was completed five years before Blickling was begun. His new master, Sir Henry Hobart, the Lord Chief Justice, seems to have given him a rather freer hand than he had been allowed by Robert Cecil. Lyminge had by then developed his skill and self-assurance to the point where his patron could trust him implicitly and give him the credit that was his due. He was permitted to incorporate his cypher RL among the stone decorations above the south entrance porch at Blickling, a privilege which the Lord Treasurer would never have countenanced at Hatfield; and the parish register of burials described him without qualification as 'the architect and builder of Blickling Hall'. It is not too fanciful to find further evidence of his greater independence in the more relaxed lines of Blickling compared to the earlier house. Hatfield's north front verges on the severe and its Long Gallery is gaunt. Blickling gained no advantage from its site – it is low-lying and hemmed in by the fosses of an earlier moat, while Hatfield was built on virgin and rising ground – but one senses immediately that its architect's intention was hospitable.

The forecourt is formed by two detached buildings enlivened by Flemish gables that roll like breakers towards the entrance front, and their curves are taken up by vast yew hedges that extend down to the road. This is the view that takes the visitor by surprise. Closing the fourth side of the rectangle, is a façade that combines colour, dignity, excitement and pageantry to a degree that was to become impossible only a few years later, when Inigo Jones rendered such indigenous creations out of date. The second Earl could refer to part of it, not unkindly, as 'Gothic'. Though Blickling owes something to Dutch and Franco-Italian influences, it is as English as a Constable. If Montacute proves that the Elizabethans could be graceful, Blickling's two untouched fronts prove that the Jacobeans could be light-hearted. All the elements of Hatfield are present here – the ogival cupolas to the corner turrets, the dominating clock-tower, the heavily decorated porch, the strap work, the pierced balconies – but they lift the spirits in a manner which Hatfield never quite succeeds in doing.

Blickling has one major fault in its design, the meanness of its two inner courts. The second hides its clutter so shamefacedly that it can only be seen from a few upper windows. They are forgotten or ignored as soon as one goes indoors. Facing the front door is a monumental staircase. It does not occupy its original position, for considerable internal rebuilding in the eighteenth century did away with the Great Hall and substituted for it a hall in the more modern sense of the term, extending across the whole inner width of the house between the east and west wings. It is from this hall that the staircase rises in two branching flights linked at their upper ends by a landing that continues

The south or entrance front. The towers are capped by ogival cupolas similar to those originally at Hatfield. This is one of several features which the two houses, both built by Robert Lyminge, had in common.

*The east front of Blickling
from a corner of the formal
garden created in the 1930s.*

The Long Gallery, famous for its elaborate plaster ceiling.

The Grand Staircase, which divides into two flights at the first landing. It is a partial reconstruction in 1760 of the original Jacobean staircase which consisted of a single flight.

the balustrade round the fourth side. Lyminge's staircase was of one branch only, and led up from the present downstairs ante-room. The existing staircase incorporates much of his original timbers and carving, but the doubling of it, the adaptation of its style and its reconstruction in a far more spectacular position, were due to Thomas Ivory, a Norfolk architect, in 1760. This was the very year when Robert Adam launched his great innovations in design which left not even Blickling untouched, and it is amazing to find that a craftsman and patrician patron of that contemptuous period could create together so proud an anachronism instead of sweeping Lyminge's work away. To mount this staircase is more impressive to the touch and tread than the ascent of the most gorgeous *treppenhaus* in a German baroque palace. The very creaking of the oak reminds one of the ingenuity of its construction; one clings to the banister-rail like a child. On each newel post stands a lovely wooden statuette, no two the same – a musketeer, a soldier in a cocked hat, a Highlander, a bearded courtier – some Lyminge's originals, some eighteenth-century improvisations on the same theme, which form an ascending sculpture gallery so romantic that the ages of Lyminge and Ivory (did the second know even the name of the first?) seem bridged by it across a hundred and fifty years.

The state-rooms on the first floor are no anticlimax to this splendid approach. They are tall, well-lit chambers which illustrate once more how happy a marriage was arranged at Blickling between the early seventeenth and late eighteenth centuries. The ceilings, doors and windows were for the most part left untouched; the Jacobean fireplaces sometimes remain, and there is a magnificent specimen in the south drawing-room, stripped to its parent oak. The walls surrendered their panelling to Gainsboroughs and Mortlake tapestries, and the floors their exposed planks to Axminster and Moorfields.

There is one room, however, which remained almost unaltered till the nineteenth century and still has the bearing of one of the noblest rooms in Britain. This is the Long Gallery, which extends a hundred and twenty feet along the greater part of the east front. Its immense plaster ceiling is renowned, its library is comparable to Longleat's, but its proportions are what make it so immediately acceptable as a great work of art. Few long galleries are later in date than Blickling, and at the moment when the awkward tradition was about to die, it at last found its justification in this room. Its unusual width makes its great length not merely tolerable but superb. Its window embrasures are large enough to accommodate a sofa. It is a room in which one can converse or work, and yet it clamours for a state ball. From its windows you look across the garden and the park towards that little white temple among the trees where this inadequately short journey began.

Wilton House
Wiltshire

IT WOULD BE RASH TO NAME any one of the great English houses still in private hands as the greatest, but Wilton must come close to it if one does not require that it be of enormous size, that it be built all of one piece and all at one time, and that the exterior be grandiloquent. Wilton demonstrates that greatness can be composed of the opposite qualities. Large it is, but not so enormous that parts of it must now be shut up, curtainless and cold. It is a unity, retaining through the centuries its four-square compactness, an almost keep-like sturdiness of plan, but each addition, reconstruction and amendment was an initiative, daring for its age. Wilton is the product of a succession of experiments and accidents which taste and time have blended into a whole.

One cannot visit Wilton without becoming aware of the firm continuity of the family, generation to generation. The Herberts, Earls of Pembroke and Montgomery, are as closely linked as any noble family in Britain, brother to brother, father to son, and it is the house which links them, for since the time of Henry VIII none but the Herberts have owned it. The evident pleasure which they take in each other's company, a pleasure that can reach back four centuries without affectation, has never frozen into ancestor-worship. On the contrary, one of the most endearing characteristics of the Herberts, which has left a significant mark on the house, is their refusal to be satisfied with the way in which things were done in their childhood. There was not only a strong streak of adventurousness in their character, carried to the point of political and military audacity, but a feeling for the arts and sciences, and a delight in the company of innovators.

The house had its origins in the great Abbey of Wilton, and part of the Abbey's knobbly stone wall has recently been uncovered, reaching high into the core of the present house. On the dissolution of the Abbey in 1544, Henry VIII presented the lands to William Herbert (1507–70), son of a distinguished Welsh family, who served François I as a soldier of fortune and was recommended by him to the English King. William married the sister of Catherine Parr, Henry's sixth Queen, and in the reigns of Edward VI, Mary and Elizabeth he became one of the most powerful figures in the country. It was he, the first Earl of Pembroke, who built the original house at Wilton as soon as the property came into his hands.

The east front, which was the entrance front till 1801. The central tower is all that survives in situ of the original Tudor house.

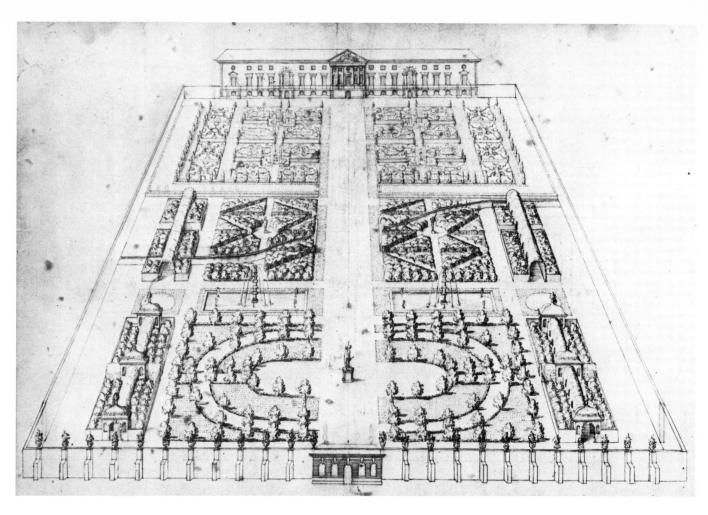

Two parts of the Tudor house survive. One is the great tower in the centre of the east front, until the early nineteenth century the main entrance to the house. Flanked today by a mixture of mid-seventeenth-century building and Wyatt's Gothick, and itself touched at parapet level by Wyatt's hand, it still outshines them both. Tall and broad, proud in its proportions, particularly of the central oriel window, it led the visitor to expect a superb house behind. He would not have been disappointed. He rode through the archway to the courtyard which still, in essentials, remains as the open centre of the house, and dismounted at an inner porch, the second of the Tudor survivals. Attributed to Holbein (but with scant authority, for Holbein died the year after the property was acquired), it stands today at the end of a long garden path, a beautiful example of the fusion between the English Gothic and Italian Renaissance styles.

It was in this house that Philip Sidney wrote his *Arcadia* and where Ben Jonson and Donne were visitors. There is adequate reason to believe that Shakespeare's *As You Like It* was first performed here, whatever one may think of the claims of William Herbert to have been the Mr W. H. of the Sonnets. But splendid as the Tudor house undoubtedly was, it alone was not enough to satisfy Philip, the fourth Earl, who succeeded his brother William in 1630. When the house was barely eighty years old, Philip pulled down the south block and erected in its place a façade and a set of rooms that have no rival for their period in the whole of English domestic architecture.

Philip's architect, it can be proudly if loosely said, was Inigo Jones. Certainly Jones was consulted, and Henrietta Maria, for whom he was then (1635) finishing the Queen's House at Greenwich, pressed the Surveyor of the Royal Works upon Wilton, for which she and the King had a deep affection. But Jones was too busy to do more than sketch an outline, and passed on the detailed work to an assistant, a Frenchman from Dieppe named Isaac de Caus. A drawing bearing de Caus' name was discovered by Mr Howard Colvin in the library of Worcester College, Oxford, and it is here reproduced. It created consternation in the world of architectural historians. For not only did it confirm beyond doubt Aubrey's hint that a Frenchman, and not the great English master Inigo Jones, was sufficiently responsible for the famous façade 'all *al Italiano*' for a contemporary elevation of it to bear his name, but it showed that the existing building is less than half that intended by its creator. There was to have been a central portico of six Corinthian columns, flanked on the far side by a wing of equivalent length. In front, aligned on this portico, extended a vast garden, a thousand feet in length by four hundred wide, with a broad central path carried over the River Nadder on a bridge as flat and unemphatic as a culvert on a modern bypass. The garden was actually constructed and maintained by an army of gardeners for over a hundred years. But of the south front only the right-hand wing was built, possibly because the outbreak of the Civil War and Philip's quarrel with the King placed the family fortunes in jeopardy.

A comparison between the de Caus elevation and the photographs of the present south front shows that nothing was lost by the curtailment of the plan.

A drawing by Isaac de Caus showing the original plan for the south front. Only the right-hand wing was completed, but the garden, crossed diagonally by the River Nadder, was actually constructed.

The south front as built by de Caus under the direction of Inigo Jones in 1635–40.

Instead, it was adapted by a stroke of genius which one feels tempted to attribute to Inigo Jones himself. The great Venetian window, which was to have been matched by another in the middle of the west wing, became the central feature; and de Caus' rather weak roof-line was lifted at each end by towers topped by pedimented pavilions. A symmetrical and perfectly composed façade was created out of the wreck of the original plan. Seldom can an architect have turned disappointment to such advantage.

The south front shields on its first storey a magnificent set of seven state-rooms, two of which, the Single and the Double Cube rooms, rise to roof height. A fire destroyed part of this block in 1647, only a few years after its completion, but Christopher Hussey has argued convincingly that it did not do as much damage as was once supposed. If we accept his thesis that the existing façade is the de Caus-Jones original (*c.* 1635–40) and that a Double Cube room was already part of the house before the fire, we need only attribute to Inigo Jones and John Webb, Jones' nephew-by-marriage, the repair and redecoration of the suite in 1648–53, and not its total reconstruction. In any case, the whole work, pre-fire and post-fire, occupied less than twenty years, inspired by Inigo Jones throughout and executed in turn by two of his ablest assistants, each of them an architect in his own right.

These seven famous rooms make on every visitor an impression of restrained richness, to which scale, colour and furnishing all contribute. To contemporaries, for whom a magnificent Jacobean house like Hatfield was barely thirty years old, Wilton must have appeared an extraordinary novelty. Italian in inspiration outside, French within, it contrives to be essentially English. The series of smaller rooms leading to the Double Cube are caskets of subdued gold. One of them, the Corner Room, occupies the south-east angle of the house, where one would expect to find a large room taking advantage of the windows on the two sides. Instead, though not the smallest of the seven, it has a warmth and intimacy rare in great foreign houses of the period, and the same is true of the Hunting Room at the opposite end. Between them, the Double Cube and the Single Cube lift the scale to palatial proportions. The first is sixty feet long by thirty wide and thirty high; the second is half the length but of the same width and height. Both are decorated by great swags of fruit and flowers, carved in wood, gilded in different shades of gold and screwed to walls of white-painted pine. The doorways, of which drawings annotated by Inigo Jones and Webb survive, the chimneypieces of Italian marble and the coved ceilings are particularly ornate, but nowhere is there the same assault on the eye as is made by the interiors of near-contemporary French houses like Vaux-le-Vicomte, where scarcely a square inch was left unenriched.

The Double Cube was redesigned after the fire to hold the magnificent series of family and royal portraits by Van Dyck, commissioned by the fourth Earl in 1632–4. They were brought down from Durham House in London, at what risk and labour one can imagine from their size, and form around the walls panels which owe almost as much to the dignity of the sitters as to the skill of the artist. How the room was otherwise furnished in the seventeenth

The fireplace and overmantel of the Double Cube Room, which remains exactly as Inigo Jones designed it. The painting by Van Dyck is of the children of Charles I.

century is not known, but the gilt and red velvet settees, the chairs and mirrors by Chippendale and William Kent, were clearly designed for the room, and although a century later in date, conform admirably to its tone and style.

By 1653 the house was complete. Still set on its square Tudor base, with carriages of increasing lightness and magnificence passing into the central courtyard through the arch of the great tower and leaving it by an equivalent arch on the opposite side, Wilton retained throughout the eighteenth century its national importance as a focus for politicians and artists and the hub of a remarkably enterprising family. There was one black sheep, the seventh Earl, a spendthrift and suspected murderer; but his brother Thomas, who succeeded him in 1683, was a man of great learning who held many high offices of state under five sovereigns and assembled the larger part of the art-collection which still enriches the house. It was his son Henry, the 'Architect Earl', who in 1736, with the help of his clerk-of-works Roger Morris, built the Palladian bridge.

James Lees-Milne rightly calls the Wilton bridge 'one of the most beautiful buildings in all England'. It crosses the little River Nadder on a level with the east front, so that the house is seen at an angle through its arches and columns, and the bridge at an angle from the southern windows, postponing the moment of delight and surprise when one walks across the lawn to view it from the side. Even if the ninth Earl had limited himself to constructing the five arches of the bridge and the balustrade, it would still have been a great achievement. But what gives it charm and originality (for it owed little to Palladio and nothing to anyone else) is the temple-portico which rises unnecessarily, extravagantly, but with the utmost grace, above it. There can be few better examples of heaviness of structure lightened by design. Mounting the mossy steps, you feel cradled in stone. The splash of the waterfall beneath, the dancing of shadows on the diamond-patterned ceiling, the enfolding arms of the balustrade, even the swan which floats obligingly below, create a mood of exhilaration and suspense. It is only afterwards that one considers in how many different variations the Palladian-bridge idea could have been carried out, and wonders at the ingenuity of the man who gave it this sublime form.

At the beginning of the nineteenth century Wilton suffered a transformation. Between 1801 and 1810, by which time relations between architect and patron had degenerated to the point of mutual insult, James Wyatt modernized the house. His work was completed by Sir Jeffrey Wyatville, his nephew. That Wyatt did not employ at Wilton the neo-classic style of which he was a greater master, but instead Gothicized it, has been much regretted. That he destroyed the hall, staircase and chapel, and displaced the 'Holbein' porch, is to our eyes unforgivable. The patently blind wall with fake doors and windows which he erected on the east side of his new approach court is one of the few architectural crimes of which Wilton remains a victim. But given all this, there is no doubt that Wyatt did the house a service by the two-storeyed cloister which he built round all four sides of the inner courtyard. It was an added convenience to a house without corridors, and is in itself a fine

The Single Cube Room, thirty feet in each dimension. It is now thought that this room survived the 1647 fire, and it therefore remains the untouched work of Inigo Jones and de Caus.

construction and a perfect setting for the Pembroke collection of classical sculpture and other works of art. Now that its walls and vaulting have been repainted in warm terracotta with grey ribs, it forms an adjunct to the house by which previous centuries would have been startled, but not, one likes to think, ashamed.

This account of Wilton has been traced chronologically. But such is the composure of the house that a description room by room, sliding the centuries in and out, would have served as well. It is a palimpsest of styles, and none except certain parts of Wyatt's contribution jars upon the rest. What blemishes it has have been masked by the taste of the sixteenth Earl. Its perfections, its superb contents, have never been shown to better advantage than they are today.

The Palladian bridge constructed in the garden by the ninth Earl of Pembroke in 1736. It was widely admired and imitated.

Felbrigg Hall
Norfolk

ARCHITECTURALLY, FEW HOUSES IN BRITAIN present a more puzzling sight than the two wings of Felbrigg meeting at a right-angle to form an L. One of them is Jacobean, the other Charles II. Only sixty years separate them, but they belong to different worlds, the first rugged, indigenous and crustacean, the second neat, classical and smart. The Jacobean wing must be one of the last houses to be built in the Elizabethan tradition, while the new wing anticipated the style which became familiar in country-houses during the next few decades. The architectural revolution is not only marvellously illustrated here, but telescoped. When William Windham built his classical wing between 1675 and 1686 he broke with the past without sweeping it away. He kept the old wing built by his father, and without fear of incongruity joined to it his bold conception of what a modern house should be.

The Jacobean wing was built in about 1620 by Thomas Windham on the site of a mediaeval house which had been in the possession of his family for nearly two hundred years. He retained the old cellars, but otherwise completely destroyed the ancestral mansion, and in its place erected a tall, wide and shallow house on four floors, of which only two are apparent from outside. The porch is advanced to form an imposing front door with two small chambers above it, and on each side a wide bay is thrust out, rising to the level of parapets pierced with the motto GLORIA DEO IN EXCELCIS. On the roof-top three groups of linked chimneys are centred above the bays. The façade is almost symmetrical, even to the equal spacing of the rainwater pipes, but the effect is rustic and homely, native to the core. Time has mellowed it more than the neighbouring wing. It was built in a haphazard mixture of brick, stone and flint, but the stucco has flaked to the great advantage of the house, revealing pink splotches of brick here and there, which gives the building a pleasantly mottled appearance, compensating for the lack of any plants growing up the walls or at its foot.

There were two main rooms extending the whole depth of the house, a hall to the left and its kitchen (now the Morning Room) to the right. A screens-passage separated them immediately inside the front door. Above, there would have been large bed-chambers and a withdrawing-room, and at roof-level a long gallery. Little of this remains today. The wing was reconstructed

and redecorated at least twice in succeeding centuries, most unfortunately in about 1840, and the 'Jacobean' rooms on the ground floor are today the least impressive, apart from their size, while the long gallery was split up into small bedrooms for servants and children, now derelict. We can be thankful that no change was made to the outside. If Felbrigg consisted in nothing but the Jacobean house, it would still be an historical work of art, a lovely last flourish to England's most traditional style.

When we turn to the new wing, all our conceptions of elegance must change. The hall of a tough and irascible squire is partnered by a gentleman's residence. The outside of the wing is late seventeenth-century, the inside mid-eighteenth, but one can take them together, for between 1680 and 1750 there was no architectural revolution comparable to that of the preceding half-century.

The wing was built for William Windham by Samwell, an architect whose name is now best remembered for this, because most of his other work has perished. It is an excellent example of English brickwork at its most cherubic. The brick is crisp and rosy red. Like its Jacobean predecessor, the wing could have stood anywhere alone. The two houses relate to each other only by touching at one corner. No attempt was made to mask their junction or to pay tribute to the earlier style in the later. Only the roof- and window-lines correspond, and even these are unapologetically approximate, for how could the broad mullions be matched to the two rows of regular windows in the new wing, or the wavy Dutch gable to the six neat dormers placed alongside it in the roof? It is like slapping down the ten of clubs beside the Queen of hearts. There is a relationship between them, but no intimacy.

In both wings there is variety, but the method by which it was achieved was greatly refined in the 1680s. In place of strong bays and exterior encrustations, there is a single shallow change of building-line at the centre emphasized by brick quoins running from near ground-level to the roof, repeated at the angles, with a string-course half-way up, a lacy cornice in place of pierced parapets, and subtly curved pediments above two of the ground-floor windows.

Alongside the wing, and at right-angles to it, separated by a strip of lawn, an orangery was built in about 1705, a well-proportioned building which today houses a lovely display of pink and red camellias. The garden proper lies at some distance from the house, bounded by brick walls and dominated by a columbarium, and stables and other outhouses were added in the eighteenth and nineteenth centuries. Great woods of beech and sweet chestnut were planted behind the house to shield it from the north wind, but to the south the view was left open to cornfields and grassland, from which emerges a mediaeval church, now separated from its village by more than a mile.

In the rear angle of the L there is a jumble of buildings. The house was not intended to be viewed from this side. No subsequent owner or architect cared what happened there, and they added corridors and a staircase haphazardly to improve the circulation. The services of the house were tucked away, leaving the two garden-fronts unimpeded. Only one change was made to either externally. On the left-hand side of the new wing a two-storey bay was attached in the eighteenth century, and the cornice (but not the string-course)

The two fronts of the house. The Jacobean house on the right contrasts strongly with the west wing, designed only sixty years later.

The Jacobean wing seen from across the park, with the eighteenth-century orangery to the left, and the stables to the right.

was carried round to disguise the alteration.

The three rooms on the ground floor of the Charles II wing run *en suite*. The first of them originally contained the staircase, but this was removed by James Paine in the early 1750s to form the present dining-room, and a new staircase hall was built behind it. The change was a great improvement. Today you emerge from the Jacobean–Victorian hall, which creates an initial disappointment by the obvious falsity of its wood and stone ornament, to enter the first of three dazzlingly beautiful rooms which combine the proportions of the seventeenth century with the glitter of the eighteenth. In two of them the plasterwork ceilings are those of the earlier period, the wall-carvings of the later, and together they form caskets for the display of scintillating furniture and pictures. Some of the latter are family portraits, others trophies of European tours. There is great richness here, no timidity in the juxtaposing of colours. The dining-room, for example, is pale lilac, against which is drawn the creamy white scrollwork of the picture-frames, square and oval. An eagle, central on the ceiling, protests furiously at the denial of the chandelier which his talons were designed to hold. Dark Victorian bronzes on the chimneypiece and wall-brackets, and richly gilded door-handles, add punctuation marks at intervals.

The dining-room, created in the 1750s by James Paine
from the earlier staircase hall. The family portraits
include Sir Joseph Ashe by Lely over the chimneypiece,
and his daughter Katherine Windham, also by Lely,
to the right of the door that leads to the
drawing-room.

Paine's Gothick library of 1754–5 is one of the finest surviving examples of the early Gothic Revival. The books are largely the collection of William Windham II (1717–61).

In the Drawing Room the wall-colour changes to scarlet, matched by the upholstery of chairs and sofas, and a dripping glass chandelier shivers slightly in the draught. The early nineteenth century, imitating the eighteenth better than it managed the Jacobean, added cornices, door-cases, curtains and a lovely Savonnerie carpet. The third room, known as the Cabinet, is the one from which Paine threw out a bay-window, closing the original windows on the left-hand wall to provide more space for the hanging of William Windham's pictures brought back from his Grand Tour of 1738–42. Of the 1680 room only the ceiling remains, rococo plasterwork and a deeply coved cornice. The red damask wall-coverings, more than two hundred years old, are as fresh as if installed yesterday, never having been exposed to anything fiercer than a north light. The pictures, including twenty-six small gouaches by Giovanni Battista Busiri of the Roman Campagna, are displayed to perfection against this rich background.

Upstairs there is a Gothic library formed by Paine in 1745 at the end of the Jacobean wing, a room darker than those below because the great western window was blanked off to provide more shelf-room for the hundreds of leather-bound books collected by the earlier Windhams. There are no modern books at all. Next door are three bedrooms still furnished in the Victorian manner. One of them has a delightful eighteenth-century Chinese wallpaper, another a fine plasterwork ceiling of the seventeenth century, and a cornice composed of garlands of white plaster flowers, below which runs a paper band of Victorian roses. How superbly certain are Victorian bedrooms compared to the rooms in which they spent their days! The bed-curtains, the white counterpanes, the plain tall wardrobes, the flowered jugs and basins, all proclaim a taste individual to its age and inhabitants, a sense of continuing family occupation which persists long after these rooms ceased to be used.

The story of Felbrigg is not only architectural. We know a great deal about the Windhams too, thanks to the researches of the last squire of Felbrigg, Robert Wyndham Ketton-Cremer, who wrote the history of his house and family a few years before his death in 1969, when he bequeathed Felbrigg and its contents to the National Trust. It is an enthralling record of a Norfolk family. One of them lost a leg at Blenheim; one, a contemporary of Pitt, became a statesman of the first rank; another was a recluse; and yet another nearly insane. But of all the Windhams whose story Ketton-Cremer told, there is one who symbolizes the rapid transformation of the house from near-mediaeval to near-modern. This was Katherine Ashe, the wife of the William Windham who built the new wing. 'She brought much happiness to Felbrigg', wrote Ketton-Cremer. 'She was gay, generous, warmhearted, a devoted wife, a loving but thoroughly sensible mother to a large family of children.' Her portrait by Lely which hangs in the dining-room shows her as a girl of seventeen on the eve of her marriage in 1669, dressed in a lilac bodice, with pearls twisted in her fair hair, plucking the blossom of an orange tree. A half-smile plays in her eyes and on her lips, as if she was already contemplating the new look which she and her husband would give to Felbrigg. Her taste was adventurous and unwavering.

138

Weston Park
Shropshire

FROM THE AIR, OR FROM THE MIDDLE OF Capability Brown's park, one sees a long line of buildings, stone mixed with brick, grey with pink, and one would know it at once as the seat of a great English family who have enjoyed and improved their property over centuries. The different sections of this train of buildings identify themselves immediately. On the left is a small eighteenth-century church with an earlier tower, in which one would expect to find the memorials of the family. In front of it, clearly an addition of the nineteenth century in its best classical style, is an orangery linked to the house by a loggia. To the right of the house is a two-storey wing faced with stone, which again illustrates the tact with which the Victorian owners of Weston increased the size of an already considerable mansion without destroying its proportions. Beyond this wing, which connects the house to it, lies a stable-block of pink brick, a larger version of the stable attached to Mompesson House in Salisbury Close, and of almost exactly the same date, 1688. Behind rises a mass of subsidiary farm and horticultural buildings, of which one, an immense Georgian barn with flanking towers, is a reminder of the agricultural revolution of the 1780s. Still farther to the right, embedded in the front edge of a wood, is a domed garden-temple which one discovers to be the creation of James Paine, one of the architects of Kedleston, in 1760–70.

But the eye is inevitably drawn back from these outriders to the house itself. It stands on a platform of terraces facing outwards to the park on three sides. From the south, one is looking at the original entrance front – a façade composed of alternate panels of brick wall and stone-framed windows, its centre emphasized by a broad band of stone rising to roof height. Arched gables at either end describe two faultless bows, each inset with an *oeil-de-boeuf*. They are joined by a pillared parapet along the flat roof, from which rise three chimney-stacks with shallow blind arches sunk into their nearer sides. The house, it could be said, owes its particular distinction to everything above the top windows. But much of its charm is also due to the colour of the brick, an orange pink, which has been accidentally enhanced by scoring it with diagonal grooves as a key for the stucco by which the house was faced in about 1825. Happily this stucco was removed in 1939, restoring the variety of colour and pattern which was an essential part of the original design.

Elizabeth, Lady Wilbraham, a portrait by Sir Peter Lely. Despite her lack of architectural training, she designed Weston Park single-handed.

Weston was built by a woman in the 1670s. Lady Wilbraham, born Elizabeth Mytton, was heiress to the earlier house which stood upon the site, and after her marriage to a Cheshire baronet, Sir Thomas Wilbraham, in 1651, they appear to have lived here almost without a break. Twenty years later, she decided to rebuild the house completely. Preserved in the library at Weston is her copy of Godfrey Richard's translation of Palladio's *First Book of Architecture* (1663). On one end-paper at the back of the book there are notes in her own clear hand headed 'For building Weston House 1671'. Scrappy as they are, and with the date apparently added as an afterthought, the notes reveal the businesslike methods of a remarkably gifted woman. One wishes that her actual drawings could have survived, but to hold this small leather-bound volume in one's hand, with the single word PALLADIO blocked in gold on its spine, is to understand something of the architectural fervour that inspired the late seventeenth century.

The south front seen from the Italian garden. The house is a remarkable adaptation of the Dutch style fashionable in the 1670s.

The style of Weston is not, however, Italian: it is Dutch. Soon after 1660 Hugh May had introduced from Holland the fashion for combining brick with stone, rounded with classical pediments, and incorporating in the exterior of a building blind arches and giant Corinthian pilasters. All these features are present at Weston except the last, and of this there is a faint reminder in the curling stone leaves above the angle-quoins from which the rounded pediments spring. But Weston is far from being a slavish imitation of any other building. May's houses, for instance, were two-storeyed and had hipped roofs. Lady Wilbraham's inventiveness is further illustrated by the quite different treatment of the church and stables. The former is roofed by most attractive barrel-vaulting, while the latter demonstrates her confident handling of the now classic English style of Wren. Her epitaph is on a tablet in the church, but her true memorial lies in this group of three buildings upon which she lavished so much art and affection.

Apart from the building of the orangery and east wing, the chief alteration subsequently made to the house was the removal of the entrance from the south to the east side in 1865. Why this was done is not quite clear, unless it was to bring sunlight into all the main living-rooms, but retrospectively it is seen as a fortunate change, for the bulky *porte-cochère*, which the Victorians attached to their houses as much to impress their guests as to shelter them, was placed against the east front instead of the architecturally more important south front. It also left its mark on the inside of the house. The library became the hall, the hall the drawing-room, and the drawing-room and breakfast-room were combined to form the present library. The staircase was reconstructed in marble in about 1900, and the inner courtyard was covered in to form billiard and smoking rooms. The main reception rooms run along the south front, opening one into the other, each with separate access from the hall. These three rooms – tapestry-room, drawing-room and library – are in their different ways rooms of great charm. The first owes its name to beautiful rose-pink Gobelin tapestries which were made for a room on the upper floor but have been splendidly adapted to the walls of this corner room on the terrace level. The other two are long but intimate rooms, enlivened by internal

The drawing-room, with the library beyond. Before the entrance was moved, this was the hall, with the front door on the left.

pillars. The oval ceiling of the drawing-room and the rich bindings in the library create exactly that difference of texture and play of light needed to give them variety.

It was in these rooms that Disraeli, the ageing Prime Minister, consoled himself for the loss of his wife by the company of Selina, Countess of Bradford. In the last eight years of his life he daily sought her company and wrote her 1,100 letters, sometimes three on a single day when he was to see her that very evening. It was an innocent affair, although the style of the letters, romantic and sometimes desperate for her affection, could suggest otherwise until one remembers their ages: Disraeli was sixty-eight when he formed this new attachment, and Lady Bradford, though fifteen years younger, was already a grandmother. The relationship was accepted by the Earl of Bradford, then Master of the Horse, and one of the reasons could be that his wife was clearly a little bored by it after the compliment had lost its edge.

To the two remarkable women with whose names Weston will always be associated, should now be added a third, the present Countess of Bradford. She has transformed the centre of the house from what could have been a mausoleum of Victorian taste into inner halls and rooms as light-hearted as a conservatory. Weston has not only survived as a superb example of Restoration architecture: it is also a model of adaptation to our present needs and tastes.

Erddig
Clwyd

ERDDIG (FOR THOSE WHO PREFER IT, the English name is Erthig) confronted the National Trust with a major problem in conservation, and by a curious paradox it has been saved by the very chances which menaced it. Local coal-workings had so undermined the house that the Coal Board awarded the Trust £120,000 in compensation. Then the town of Wrexham, only two miles away, needed space for new housing, and the Trust was able to sell sixty-four acres of a relatively unimportant part of the park for the colossal sum of £1,115,000, at a moment when building-land values reached their peak in 1973. Adding the two sums together, the Trust now had enough money to restore a major house which was in danger of falling apart, and to save a splendid park by sacrificing a corner of it. In addition, the garden, which had lost its character through neglect, was replanted and its walls rebuilt. When all this had been done, a substantial balance remained for the future maintenance of the property.

The structure of the house was sturdy enough to survive much ill-treatment. The subsidence of the coal-mine had caused one wing to sink three feet and the other five feet, but from outside you would scarcely notice that Erddig has been the victim of a minor earthquake. The main damage was internal. The stresses had so distorted the roof that nothing but total rebuilding, as much as possible with the original timbers, could restore it, and until this was done, the roof opened at the seams to allow rainwater to stream down the interior walls and cause the near-collapse of some of the ceilings.

When the National Trust first surveyed the property, it was in a dreadful state. Exquisite furniture of the seventeenth and eighteenth centuries was exposed to damp and the direct drip of rain; the walls and ceilings were discoloured, the fabrics in some cases saturated, the rooms left for months on end undusted, and sheep instead of guests had been welcomed in the saloon. It is astonishing that the damage was not irreparable. But the delicacy of furniture of this quality conceals the craftsmanship of its construction. More harm, indeed, could have been done to it by decades of central heating. Many pieces needed careful restoration, notably the showpiece of the house, a magnificent 1720 bed finely worked in Chinese silks, which lay exposed to the weather in a room where pit-props prevented the total collapse of the ceiling.

The State Bed, the finest piece of furniture at Erddig, and one of the most splendid in Britain. It was made in 1720, largely of Chinese silk, and has survived exposure to the weather to be restored to its original glory by the Victoria and Albert Museum.

In other cases the furniture required little more than a generous application of polish. The porcelain and silver remain unharmed by neglect, but the fabrics needed more attention. Since the shutters had been closed for years, no damage had been done to them by sunlight, but several years' work, and the cannibalization of some parts of the curtains, were needed to restore them.

Restoration of the structure and contents was the first obvious duty of the National Trust, but they were also faced with the problem of what character to give the house. The Yorke family, who had owned Erddig for over two hundred years, had acquired much and never thrown anything away, and the rooms had in some cases been overloaded with later furniture and ephemeral ornaments which ill-suited the refined décor and possessions of their eighteenth-century predecessors. A Victorian sofa known as a *confidante* looks

ungainly alongside a Boulle dressing-table and to some extent spoils the look of a room, and although the house contains no pictures of high quality, ancestral portraits are not improved by placing them alongside nineteenth-century prints in ill-fitting frames. A pile of tatty 1920-ish books on a rent-table may convey a note of domestic casualness, but are inharmonious. On the other hand, a house is a palimpsest, the record of progressive generations, and if it is to be presented truthfully, changing tastes and resources must be allowed to leave their mark. It would have been tempting to prettify all the rooms, restoring them to the way they looked when the Yorkes first occupied them. The Tapestry Room has been cleared of later accretions, but other rooms have been left more or less as they developed. The Trust decided to show a house which illustrates three centuries of continuous occupation, and the interest of Erddig gains greatly from this method.

One peculiarity of Erddig makes this treatment specially appropriate. The Yorkes had a quite exceptional relationship with their servants. They were not a distinguished family. None of them won more than local eminence, and their lives centred on the house and its estate. Their large indoor and outdoor staffs meant as much to them as their guests, and they treated them not with kindness merely, but with affection and esteem. Their portraits in oil, painted in the eighteenth century by journeymen for two guineas apiece, were hung in the servants' hall as naturally·as the family's were hung in the drawing-room, and when photography replaced painting, the custom was continued until quite recent times. Doggerel verses, varying little in style from the early eighteenth to the early twentieth centuries, were attached to the paintings and photographs to extol the merits of generations of carpenters, cooks, house-maids, coachmen and gardeners:

> *Upon the portly frame we look*
> *Of one who was our former cook*

or

> *Within this frame, sedate and staid,*
> *Is Erthig's worthy parlour maid,*
> *Wife of our good head-gardener here,*
> *The name whose portrait figures near.*

At intervals, like a school-group, the whole staff would be assembled on the outside steps and photographed together, so that one can trace the rise of some of them from scullery-maid to lady's-maid, from boot-boy to butler, over periods extending sometimes to fifty years.

We know not only what the servants looked like, and from their dress, attitudes and expression, the status they occupied in the hierarchy of the servants' hall, but we can see the very places where they slept and worked. Erddig must be one of the very few houses in Britain to show to the public the maids' bedrooms, and the whole range of domestic offices from kitchen to the butler's pantry. Outside, grouped around it like a village, we can visit the many workshops which made the estate virtually self-supporting. There is the stable-yard, with its loose-boxes and carriages, early bicycles and early cars. A joiner's shop, the sawpit, the blacksmith's shop and wagon-shed, the lime-yard, the laundry and the bakehouse. Many of these are still equipped with the heavy machinery that was introduced just before the First World War (if one had to choose a central date for this part of Erddig, it would be about 1910), and several of them have been restored to working order and supply the house and estate buildings with the materials for their maintenance and repair, and home-baked bread for the tourists. It is a bundling-together of cottage industries, a revivification of a way of life which the most elderly of local people can still distantly remember.

To return to the house itself. The central block was built between 1684 and 1689 by Thomas Webb, a local master-mason, for Joshua Edisburg, who lost most of his money and sold Erddig to John Meller, a London lawyer, in 1716. It was Meller who added the two wings and sumptuously refurnished the almost empty house. In 1733 he died a bachelor, and left the property to his nephew Simon Yorke, in whose family it remained. Philips succeeded Simons, and Simons Philips, for generations (so that one has to give them Roman numerals, like kings) until the last of them, Philip III, gave Erddig to the National Trust with nearly two thousand acres of land in 1973.

It is a brick-built house, stone-faced in 1772–3 on the entrance front where it was exposed to the prevailing wind. A drawing dated 1713 shows its original appearance when it was wingless and handsomer than it appears today, a strong cupola rising from the roof like that at Belton. Since the stone facing was added, the house from this side seems dull more than ugly, the wings

The portrait of the Erddig carpenter in 1830, one of a series of paintings which the Yorke family commissioned to commemorate several generations of their servants.

withdrawn and featureless to the point of insipidity, and the only relief from austerity is a pediment and a curving outside staircase. Looking over the park from the front door, one can see the winding-gear of Bersham Colliery, which nearly wrecked the house (it is the only coal-mine still operating in North Wales), and beyond it the huge slag-heap of which the table-topped summit coincides from this angle exactly with the line of the distant hills. If it were a natural feature covered with vegetation, as one day it will be, it would excite admiration. As it is, it is an extraordinarily blunt termination to the sylvan view across the park.

When one walks round the house to the garden side, any initial disappointment with Erddig is immediately dispelled. Here the brick was left unfaced, the wings unrecessed, and we have a long building of great elegance and charm, totally different in character from the entrance front. Pleasant variations were introduced in it, like the pair of oval windows inserted in both wings (a bucolic reminder of Wren's Hampton Court), and a tiny five-column balustrade in the centre of the roof.

Outwards from it extends the garden. When the National Trust acquired the property it was overgrown and in total disarray, the long encircling wall broken in many places, the gravel paths obliterated, the two long fish-ponds or 'canals' silted up and their margins wavering to decay, and the beeches which extended the lime-avenue towards the house well past their prime. The only gardeners were seven sheep. Now the garden has been restored to something like its appearance in 1740, new trees planted regularly, and the ponds dredged. Apart from the old limes, it is a garden refashioned from vestigial relics, and when mature, it will recreate almost exactly the view from the house, and of the house, which once complemented each other perfectly.

Erddig is a phenomenon. Architecturally it is no masterpiece, but it deserves to be numbered among the great houses because it is a rare survival of something that was once normal. Individually some of its contents, like the great oyster-white bed and the gilt pier-glasses, could take their place in the finest rooms illustrated in this book. Individually, too, a few rooms, like the Tapestry Room, the Chinese Room and the chapel, are excellent examples of their kind. But what make the house fascinating to the visitor are its accretions – the hugger-mugger of its later furniture, the workshops, the portraits, and the sense of continuous occupation by all those Simons, all those Philips, who lived in it and loved it for nearly two centuries and a half.

The garden front, built c. 1683, with the formal pond, or 'canal', of a decade later.

Belton House
Lincolnshire

IN THE GARDEN AT BELTON, drawing out the date of the house effortlessly at either end, are a Norman church and an early-Victorian orangery. The latter, with its slim vertical lines and well-proportioned statuary on the roof, does no discredit to the superb house across the lawn. But the church is even better, not so much for its pleasantly chunky exterior as for the memorials which it contains. A visit to Belton might well begin here. Family tombs have a way of becoming monotonous with their cold marble and unfailingly eulogistic inscriptions. But the Belton memorials are so continuous, generation to generation for nearly three hundred and fifty years, that their cumulative message of mingled affection and pride is deeply impressive.

Here is the founder of the family fortunes, a Jacobean lawyer, Richard Brownlow (1555–1638), stiff in his niche and ruff; here his son and daughter-in-law, marble hands clasped everlastingly in mutual consolation for their childless marriage; here the lovely tablet to the memory of Sir John Brownlow (1660–97), to whom no statue was raised since it was enough to point to 'the testimony of his noble house which he built from the ground'; here Speaker Cust's memorial, the House of Commons mace peeping out discreetly from behind a shield; Lord Tyrconnel, the early eighteenth-century owner of Belton, comes next, surrounded by as delightful a canopy as ever framed a Georgian fireplace: and then succeeding Earls and Barons Brownlow attended by heavily draped ladies in attitudes of mourning or pointing the way to heaven, or more directly represented by recumbent effigies in crusader-like poses, one with a jowled bulldog at his feet. Clearly they were proud of each other, and with reason, for each has contributed something to his country's and family's greater honour, and to the estate which binds them together across the centuries.

One meets the same people again inside the house, less solemn in their portraits than in their effigies, people with passions and prejudices as well as virtues and pedigrees, each with a taste for his or her contemporary furniture and decoration, and as prone to disappointment, enthusiasm, ambition and a desire for occasional solitude as the rest of us. But as so often, the impress of the builder on the house is the strongest of all. Not much is known of Sir John Brownlow's public life except that he was High Sheriff of Lincolnshire and

twice Member of Parliament for Grantham, but his private life glows more strongly through the mist of time. He married his cousin when they were both aged sixteen, and died before he was forty. In that short interval he had created two great legacies: a family of five beautiful daughters (his only son died of smallpox in his infancy), and one of the loveliest of houses to survive from the age of Wren.

Belton is not an original house in the sense that it introduced any new fashion in architecture. It is simply a summing-up of all that is best in the only truly vernacular style that England had produced since the late Tudors. Built with astonishing rapidity in three years (1684–7), it followed very closely the design of Clarendon House in Piccadilly, which was completed by Roger Pratt in 1647 and was demolished only the year before Belton was begun. 'Pratt's masterpiece', says Sir John Summerson, 'was the most influential house of its time among those who aimed at the grand manner ... Belton is much the finest surviving example of its class.' The contracting mason, William Stanton, is known, but the architect is not. The parallel with Clarendon House, however, is so close that any able draftsman could have drawn the plans of one from the other. The only difference between them is that the ends of the two wings have been narrowed at Belton from three windows' width to two, the main front has seven windows to Clarendon's nine, and there are equivalent changes to the number of dormers in the hipped roof. These changes make no difference to the proportions; if anything, they are even better at Belton.

The north side of the house which faces the garden is identical with the entrance front, but the former is slightly the more satisfying since it lacks the pilasters and entablature with which Wyatt framed the front door in the 1770s. If one were asked to show a stranger a single example of an English country-house at its proudest and most serene, one could not do better than lead him into the garden at Belton. Houses often have the same characteristics as different types of person of different ages. Belton exactly matches its builder's in the year of his death: a man of modest public distinction aged thirty-seven. Here is maturity without loss of vigour; no trace of pompousness, and little femininity; pride, certainly, in the display of arms in the pediments, but no attempt whatever to daunt the stranger – the deeply indented wings are as companionable as the arms of a chair. This effect is achieved with the minimum of fuss. Partly it is due to the beautifully weathered ashlar from the nearby Ancaster quarry, and on the south side to the lacy wrought-iron gates and railings attributed to Thomas Robinson, *c.* 1710; but mainly it is a lesson in balance and proportion, that indefinable quality, recognized when seen, that will be discussed later in the account of Antony, a Cornish house that shares many of Belton's merits. The exterior has been contrasted with the interior and called 'austere'. The description could not be less apt. Austerity implies that there has been no attempt to please. Belton has no other aim in view, and by the subtlest methods it succeeds brilliantly.

Within the house we find the same friendliness. The 'public' rooms still seem private. The ceilings are for the most part of only moderate height and the rooms are nowhere of dimensions that would fit them for only the grandest

The north, or garden front, which is almost identical with the entrance front and has remained unaltered since the house was built in 1684–7.

*The entrance front of Belton from the
south-west. The pilasters and entablature
to the front door were added by Wyatt in
1777.*

*The Chinese Bedroom furnished according
to fashionable eighteenth-century taste.
The walls are hung with hand-painted
paper, and the bed-hangings are of
finely wrought Chinese silk.*

occasions. There are bedrooms so superbly furnished that their contents would be accepted gratefully by any museum tomorrow, but they could be slept in tonight. In the Saloon, the drawing-room and particularly the small tapestry-room, the richness of the furniture, walls, ceilings and works of art is subdued to the point where each demands examination in turn instead of competing against each other in a blaze of vainglory. One can still imagine them as they were in the early eighteenth century, occupied by Sir John's formidable widow and her five marriageable daughters. Once, it is said, the girls were giving an unsanctioned tea-party in an upper room at Belton when they heard their mother's footsteps approaching. There was only one thing to do. The whole tea-service – unemptied cups, tea-pot, table-cloth, cakes – was tossed out of the window just in time.

The impression which Belton makes today is not inconsistent with the spirit of these unmanageable girls. It is a light-hearted house. At the same time it is exquisite in its detail. From the resplendently gilded greyhound which flashes from the cupola above the house to its smaller companions on the brass door-plates in almost every downstairs room, it bears the stamp of family pride and care. There is nothing lavish about Grinling Gibbons' festoons and picture-surrounds in the hall, Saloon, chapel-gallery and elsewhere. They are simple, delicate works of art. That they should form the most important decorations at Belton is symptomatic of its whole character – gentle, undemonstrative, fanciful and yet supremely confident.

A detail of the wood-carvings by Grinling Gibbons, set against the wainscoting of the chapel-gallery.

Uppark
Sussex

THE WORD UPPARK IS PRONOUNCED with equal stress on both syllables, as if to distinguish it from Downpark which lies in the valley behind, and to proclaim, with no risk of misunderstanding, that this is a house in a park on top of a hill. The house is as straightforward as its name. It rises on the edge of an escarpment of the downs, looking southwards towards the sea over a huge landscape of sliding, dipping and crossing hills, which are so varied by their contours and woods that even Humphrey Repton conceded that any addition would be superfluous. But this stupendous view comes as a surprise. The visitor climbs the hill to approach the house from the north, where trees, outbuildings and the bulk of the house itself conceal the view and lead him to suppose that there will be a formal flattish garden on the far side. He comes round the corner of the house to discover the secret of its situation. There is no garden on this side. Instead, the open parkland, once cropped by deer and now by sheep and cattle, runs up to the very doorstep. Previously there was an oval pond in front of the house, and still earlier a small *parterre*, but later generations have tacitly agreed that the view should be as unimpeded as its approach is secret. Where one had expected to find at most a barn, thrust out by its lane into the middle of downland, one finds a palace. It could not be quieter nor seemingly more remote. It stands beautiful and compact, as if all civilization had led up to this point in space and time, and there was no object in going further.

Turning round to face the house from the park, one sees an impressive façade of brick and stone, simple in its proportions but boldly decorated. The arms of Fetherstonhaugh are thickly encrusted on the tympanum of the pediment, and festoons of stone flowers hang round the door and the window above it. Most remarkably and effectively, the modillions (brackets) under the cornices of roof and pediment are richly ornamented. It is this combination of strong exterior decoration with the plain stone borders to the windows that gives the house its masculine character. For while it is immensely elegant, there is no fuss or sentimental delicacy in any part of it. It represents a style that is fully mature, owing something to the Netherlands, but immediately recognizable as English of the Restoration period.

The architect is not known. But we do know that Uppark was built about

The south and east fronts seen from the park.

1690 for Ford, Lord Grey of Werke, later Earl of Tankerville. It is normal for English families to prefer their more disreputable ancestors to the respectable, but Lord Grey is an exception. He was a mean man, a seducer, a political turncoat and a trickster. 'Cold Caleb', Dryden called him, 'below the dignity of verse.' But he did build Uppark, and for that much can be forgiven him. An earlier family house had stood upon the site, of which some masonry survives in the basement, and the park was already mature when Celia Fiennes rode this way in 1694, soon after the house had been completed. 'I went to Chichester', she wrote, 'through a very fine Parke of the Lord Tankervailes, stately woods and shady tall trees for at least 2 mile: in the middle stands his house which is new built, square, 9 windows in the front and seven in the sides, brickwork with freestone coynes and windows: its in the midst of fine gardens, gravell and green walks and bowling green.' When she saw it, and until the early nineteenth century, the entrance was on the east side. The first sight of the house and the view to the south was therefore originally obtained from a distance, along the downs from the east, and one can be forgiven for wishing that it was still so. But Repton considered that nobody would want to look out of his bedroom window on to a forecourt, and switched the entrance to the north front – the 'useful' front, as he called it – where a huddle of domestic buildings already existed and he could screen them with a new Doric portico. In his defence it can be said that the original architect had taken little trouble about this façade, and that Repton destroyed nothing. Indeed, the change of front has made possible a charming lawn on the east side, from which the brick and stone rise even more effectively than from the adjoining park.

Each of its past owners has left his or her distinctive mark upon it. Only six generations have lived in it as their home since the time of its building. Lord Tankerville's grandson sold the estate in 1746 to Matthew Fetherstonhaugh, a youth from a Northumberland family, who inherited a vast fortune and bought a baronetcy to go with the place. It is to Sir Matthew and his wife Sarah Lethieullier that we owe the eighteenth-century decoration of the main rooms. The chief of them, the Saloon, is a double-cube room comparable to that at Wilton, although a century later in date and immeasurably lighter in style. For while in the Wilton room Inigo Jones and Webb had made use of heavy doorways and ornate swags against the walls, the decoration of the Uppark Saloon is of a gossamer fragility. Its colour is ivory, spangled with dull gold. The doorways, the reveals of the windows, the surrounds of the pictures and the ceiling coves are fondled by straying tendrils of gilded wood, in complete contrast to the virile decoration of the stonework on the wall outside. The Saloon is on the ground floor of the house, but its slight elevation on the basement podium and the sharp drop of the parkland outside the windows give the impression of a first-storey room, like the Double Cube at Wilton. Through these windows the sun streams in upon a carpet patterned like a garden-bed, while the curtains, drawn up into thick flounces during the daytime, are of French brocade, carefully cleaned and reconditioned.

Sir Matthew's only son, Sir Harry Fetherstonhaugh, was born in the house and succeeded to the estate in 1774 at the age of twenty. He lived there for ninety-two years. He was the buck of the family, the close friend of the Prince Regent, who often used to drive over from the Brighton Pavilion to enjoy Sir Harry's excellent table and string of race-horses. But Sir Harry's name will always be connected with two women, one his mistress, the other his wife. The mistress was none other than Emma Hart, later Lady Hamilton. When Sir Harry knew her, she was only sixteen years old. The daughter of a Cheshire blacksmith, she had come to London and found employment first as a maid-servant and then as a model in a 'Temple of Hymen' run by a quack doctor. Emma Hamilton was a girl of startling physical attractions, and Sir Harry installed her for a year at Uppark (whether in the actual house or not is uncertain, for his mother was living there at the time), and then as abruptly rejected her.

The central part of the south front, a beautiful façade of brick and stone, with the arms of Fetherstonhaugh boldly carved in the pediment above the upper windows.

Sir Harry's marriage was even more spectacular. In 1825, when he was over seventy, he walked one day along the terrace west of the house and heard a girl singing in the dairy. Her name was Mary Ann Bullock. Sir Harry made her acquaintance, and soon afterwards proposed. 'But do not answer me now,' he said. 'If you will have me, cut a slice out of the leg of mutton that is coming up for my dinner today.' When the mutton arrived, the slice was cut. The dairy still survives, a graceful little pavilion as light as buttermilk itself, at the end of the grass terrace. The dairymaid lived at Uppark as Lady Fetherstonhaugh until her death in 1875.

The remarkable history of Uppark had one further surprise in store. In the 1880s, a boy of fourteen, the son of the housekeeper, sat down at the kitchen table and began his first literary composition, a daily newspaper called *The Uppark Alarmist*. The boy was H. G. Wells. 'The place had a great effect on me,' he wrote in his autobiography. 'It retained a vitality that altogether overshadowed the insignificant ebbing trickle of upstairs life.' No other house in England is quite like it for the perfect condition of its eighteenth-century furnishings and hangings. The memories of all that has happened there are treasured as much as the works of art. An atmosphere of Elysian calm pervades its quiet rooms and downland park.

Petworth House
Sussex

THIS IS ONE OF THE VERY FEW GREAT HOUSES in England which is supposed to have been strongly influenced by French architecture. Horace Walpole could speak of it as being 'in the style of the Tuileries', and in our own times Sir John Summerson called it 'conspicuously French' and Christopher Hussey 'a singular instance of French influence'. Except in the decoration of the centre and wings of the main façade, this influence is not now very apparent. To recapture its 'foreignness', one must look at the painting identified by Sir Anthony Blunt at Belvoir, showing the façade as it must have appeared soon after its completion in 1696. That this was not a fanciful reconstruction is proved by a very similar sketch which peeps out between the huge figures of Laguerre's wall-paintings on the Grand Staircase. Both show a balustrade surmounting a dome in the centre of the front. The balustrade is crowned by urns, and at the foot of the dome, on the parapet of the main roof-line, stand gesticulating statues, which are repeated on the parapets of the two wings. Ten more urns are spaced between the three groups. All this has now disappeared. It is supposed that a serious fire early in 1714 destroyed the dome and gutted much of the southern part of the house, and although the main fabric was soon rebuilt, the dome was not, and the statues and urns were never replaced.

By accident, therefore, Petworth was anglicized, and its only formal front simplified to the point of plainness. But it has three distinct characters – from the long, middle and short distance. You can see its full extent from over a mile away, across the lake, and from here it appears as a long grey house, its roof-line straight from end to end, punctuated only by regularly spaced chimneys. Its forty-two tall windows form two main floors. Its length and paleness are the first most obvious impressions. The second is its setting, for few parks curtsey so gracefully towards the house or cushion it so sympathetically. A rounded tree-covered knoll, partly artificial, dips from the north-west to flatten out at exactly the point where the podium of the house begins. The lake is serpentine, enlarged by Capability Brown between 1751 and 1757, and it is speckled with little islands on which stand great urns of stone or a single dripping willow. Its verge is neither marshy nor diked, but firmly drawn by low mossy banks, beyond which the uninterrupted parkland

The great house of the Duke of Somerset as it appeared in about 1700. Since this picture (now at Belvoir) was painted, the central dome and statues on the roof have gone, and the entrance was switched to the other side of the house.

OPPOSITE *The main front of Petworth House seen from its park. The roof-line is flat, and the blunted tower on the left is that of the village church, which stands some way behind the house.*

OVERLEAF LEFT *The Double Cube Room at Wilton, one of the most famous rooms in Britain. It retains all the original decorations by Inigo Jones and John Webb, but some of the furniture is later. The painting by Van Dyck at the far end is one of the Herbert family, and is his largest conversation piece.*

OVERLEAF RIGHT *The Chinese Bedroom at Felbrigg Hall was designed by James Paine, who hung the walls with the lovely Chinese wallpaper in about 1751.*

rises to the house, and herds of deer and sheep roam as far as the very windows.

As you stand on the nearer side of the lake, the details of the façade cannot yet be discerned. This therefore is its plainest aspect, and the point at which one most regrets the loss of the centre-piece. Luckily one can replace it in imagination, for the blunted tower of Petworth Church, which rises well behind the house, can be manoeuvred by walking right or left to a position above the exact centre of the roof. One cannot, however, replace the gates and circular drive shown in the Belvoir picture, for the entrance was switched in the nineteenth century to the east side, between the church and the house, and from this distance there is nothing beyond the faint rustication of the three main bays and their scribbled decoration to indicate that the house has a focal point at all.

From the foot of the terrace the whole façade springs to life. Now one sees the variation of its stonework – rough, local stone for the main walls, Portland for the wings and centre, the firm surrounds for the doors and windows, the heavy cornice, the beautifully spaced balusters above it, the francophil busts and carvings above nine of the ground-floor windows, the subtle projection of the wings, the terrace and the stone seats along it. Look at either wing in isolation, and you will see that the attribution of French influence is justified and the charge of excessive plainness is not. All that is missing from a 'normal' house of the period, French or English, are giant pilasters in place of the modest rainwater pipes, and some emphasis for the central doorway.

Petworth, in proportion to its length and height, is a narrow house, only two rooms thick, and there was no space within it for the usual services. These are contained in loosely knit blocks behind and parallel to the main house, joined to it below ground by tunnels through which servants trundled food and fuel, and above ground by an archway constructed in the last century. The entrance drive now runs directly out of the little town of Petworth between those two blocks, and the whole building on this side is tightly belted in by a high wall dividing it from the busy streets immediately outside. This arrangement, odd for so patrician a house, has an historical origin. A nobleman's castle stood here since at least the twelfth century, when it came into the possession of the great Percy family, later Earls of Northumberland, and it would have been normal for the town-houses to huddle close beneath the castle walls. It was several times rebuilt, but it kept its site and part of its massive structure. Some of the cellars of the present Petworth are semi-cylindrical caverns of near-Roman size and stubbornness, and the main walls of the chapel are those of the fourteenth century.

In 1682 Petworth passed by marriage from the Percies to the sixth Duke of Somerset, and it is to him, 'the Proud Duke', that we owe by far the larger part of the existing house.

He started rebuilding it with his wife's fortune in 1688. Basically its plan is simple. Nine state-rooms lead one into the other along the front facing the park, and are matched by a succession of rooms of similar size behind. Some of them were refashioned after the fire of 1714 or in later centuries, adding

OPPOSITE *The magnificent centre-piece of the Grinling Gibbons Room in Petworth House. The portrait of Henry VIII is framed by swags of fruit and flowers executed by the famous seventeenth-century carver.*

thereby to the interest and continuity of Petworth's long history. Three of them are of quite outstanding importance in the development of English art. These are: the Marble Hall, the Grinling Gibbons Room, and the chapel.

The Marble Hall lies in the centre of the west front, and was the original entrance hall. Although it is strongly embellished, it is made to appear simple by its size, its lambency and its emptiness. Its tones are white and pale green. In each wall there is a doorway. The centre one, opposite the glass park door, leads through a wide opening to the state dining-room, with a Roman statue in a shadowed apse on each side of it. The floor is of green, black and white marble, and the ceiling plain. Two dove-grey fireplaces face each other from the north and south walls. All this gives the room its gossamer coolness, but its richness comes from the carving around the doors, above the fireplaces and along the cornice. There is nothing timid about this carving, all of which was the work of John Selden, the Duke's estate carver who is not known to have worked elsewhere than at Petworth. To the eighteenth century it might have appeared gross. The egg and tongue moulding to the cornice, for example, and the acanthus brackets that project between it and the ceiling, are of unusual size, but they are delicate in their total impression because their scale is

The overmantel of the Marble Hall. The unicorn and the bull were the supporters of the arms of the Duke of Somerset, and they were carved by John Selden, the Duke's estate carpenter.

Part of the wall-carving by Grinling Gibbons in the room named after him. In the opinion of Horace Walpole, it was the famous carver's masterpiece. Every part of it is executed in limewood.

exactly right for the room. The framing round the doors and windows is broad and fluffy, like intertwined woollen fillets. The best of all are the surrounds of the fireplaces and the Duke's beasts, a bull and a unicorn, reclining above them on either side of his escutcheon. These splendid animals, angry in their precarious and unalterable positions, are carved in the round, but they are part of the architecture of the room, not ornaments placed around it. What a wonderful entrance it made!

To the north, through the little dining-room, lies Petworth's showpiece, the Grinling Gibbons Room. It does not arouse in the visitor the same immediate delight as many of the others, for its overall colour is parchment brown, and its proportions (sixty feet long by twenty-four wide and twenty high) are more those of a gallery than a room. Moreover, the burden of carving on the east wall is first seen from one end, and it consequently appears scabby in the mass. It is almost as if Grinling Gibbons, working at great pressure in his London studio (he was simultaneously busy on his designs for Hampton Court and the library at Trinity College, Cambridge), had concentrated on the individual carvings without considering carefully their total effect. Exquisite in detail, they are rather burdensome in bulk, in direct contrast to the Marble Hall, where the detail is heavy but the effect light. The panels behind the carvings were once painted white, but the paint was stripped off in about 1870 by Lord Leconfield. It was then thought an improvement, but the apparent greater delicacy of Jonathan Ritson's brooch-like traceries against the white cove of the ceiling makes one wonder whether Gibbons' finer work would not benefit by the same background.

His scheme for the room was to supply three-sided frames for seven large portraits – a pair on each side of Henry VIII and a single portrait at either end of the room, and smaller pictures above the four doors. Each picture was surmounted by an immensely elaborate composition in carved limewood, from which depended drops or swags composed of flowers, game, fruit and other objects. The light from the four west windows falls full on the main wall, but although one can see the lower parts of the drops clearly, the upper parts and overpieces are placed too high for close inspection; yet photographs show that they were executed as carefully as if they could be seen at eye-level. Some of the carving is biscuit-thin, and in this single material Gibbons contrived with brilliant virtuosity the effect of every other – skin and feathers, shell and scales, leaf and petal, basketwork, violin strings, lace, the ribbon and metal of the Duke's coronet and Garter, the flesh of fruit and the flesh of cherubs' cheeks. Nothing is so dead as his dead birds, nothing so alive as his fluttering doves. Most of the carving is three-dimensional, but as the planes recede towards the wall, it is flattened to give the effect of even greater depth. Thus in flower-filled baskets, the ribs of the basket stand clear of the nearest flowers, while those behind are merely suggested by the point of a leaf, a half-hidden stem, but nothing seems crushed. The room is a museum of such artifices, and as such it should be studied, piece by piece.

In the chapel a glorious effect is achieved by placing late seventeenth-century gilded woodwork against thirteenth-century stone. The Early English

The Grinling Gibbons Room, dominated centrally by the portrait of Henry VIII after Holbein.

The mediaeval chapel at Petworth was redecorated in the 1690s by the 6th Duke of Somerset, who added the plaster ceiling and the gallery above the entrance. The carvings were probably made by Selden in the early eighteenth century.

arcades on each side are those of the Percies' chapel; the stalls, altar-rail, reredos, gallery and ceiling were added by the Duke of Somerset in 1690–2. The floor of the chapel is eight steps below that of the main house, the gallery an equal height above it, and the variety of the walls and furnishings is made the more impressive by the changes in level. You look down upon the chapel before entering it, and then look up from the altar steps to the splendidly baroque proscenium of painted wood above the gallery. The huge east window is sparsely filled by armorial glass, and in daylight it is so dazzling that the magnolia outside the window is seen more clearly than the altar piece within it. This is the only disturbing feature of a room which in its proportions, associations, ornament and muted colour is one of the most attractive in the house and the only one which frankly proclaims its ancient origins.

Among the later changes, one room in particular is a lovely example of its period. This is the White and Gold Room, a sitting-room in the private part of the house. It was redecorated in the mid-eighteenth century by Alicia Maria, Countess of Egremont, and is thought to be the room in Turner's *Drawing Room at Petworth*, now in the National Gallery in London. While its dimensions are not exactly those of a cube, it gives that satisfying impression. The basic colour of the panelled walls is faded ivory, against which are applied thin ribs and tendrils of gilded wood, nearer the rococo in style than Robert Adam, and as such rather an anachronism for their date. The nineteenth-century chandelier of ormolu and Rockingham porcelain is a beautiful piece of work, fully worthy of the Chippendale mirror above the fireplace, which must surely have been made for the room or the room for it. The third colour (after ivory and gilt) is the pale blue of the curtains, chair-coverings and flounces of the tables on each side of the fireplace, and a fourth, the pinks of the carpet, a late eighteenth-century English design in the Aubusson manner. As a colour scheme, and for its subtle mixture of style and period, this sitting-room is a wonderful composition.

Looking back on Petworth, one cannot escape the conclusion that it is a strange house. Its architecture, site and arrangements have a certain awkwardness. The confusion of the rooms on the east side of the main floor and of the bedrooms above it, together with the wanderings of the staircases and corridors between them, betray the lack of any thought-out plan, or the sacrifice of internal convenience to outside appearance on the west front and to historical chance on the east. Its architect, if there ever was one in the full sense, is unknown. But it contains rooms and a magnificent art-collection which are among the great glories of England. You can stand beside the picture which Turner, the favourite guest of the third Earl of Egremont, painted of its park in 1829, and by glancing out the window see the same view which he captured so brilliantly on the canvas. Then, looking back along the receding vista of doors, you find yourself transplanted a further one hundred and forty years back to the days of the Proud Duke, whose patronage of artists left a legacy no less enduring.

Mompesson House
Salisbury, Wiltshire

HERE IS THE SMALLEST HOUSE DESCRIBED IN THIS BOOK, and if one excepts Brighton Pavilion, the only town-house. Yet in Salisbury Close you have no feeling of being in the centre of a town. It is a village green on which has risen unexpectedly the tallest and one of the loveliest of English cathedrals. The houses which surround it on the north side are toylike beside the great grey church, and their architecture, as if by the common consent of seven centuries, has remained modest and almost rural. The effect is heightened by the green lawns which run up to the very foot of the cathedral walls (we owe this to Wyatt, who overcame heaven knows what opposition to the removal of the gravestones) and by the dominant cherry-pink brick in which many of the Canons' houses were reconstructed. The general layout of the Close has remained unchanged since the Middle Ages, but immediately after the Civil War it became a rubbish dump, a children's playground, a market-place and a butchers' slaughterhouse. Its present appearance dates from roughly the turn of the seventeenth century, when the mess was cleared up and Wren was called in to advise. At the same period the finest house of them all, Mompesson House on the north side of Choristers' Green, was given its second and almost final form.

Around this square of grass is ranged an exhibition of English architecture from the fourteenth to the eighteenth century. Only one house, Mompesson itself, could be called a masterpiece, but collectively there is no lovelier sight in Britain, except perhaps the Great Court at Trinity College, Cambridge, which owes its harmony to the same haphazard fusion of several English styles. No attempt was made by the cathedral authorities of those days to impose a common building or roof-line. The little houses sit good-naturedly side by side, some canonical, some secular, one a former schoolhouse, another the residence of its headmaster; a few hide their Gothic muddle behind a decent frame of Georgian brick, others are patched with flints and brick-nogging; some are lit by windows arched and cusped, some with sashes and cornices; there are front doors of every variety, and gardens everywhere.

From this attractive jumble Mompesson House stands out with serene dignity. It is princess of the Green, as the cathedral is queen of the Close. But it does not dominate the others snobbishly. True, it is the only one faced with

stone, and the only one with an imposing doorway, iron railings and gate-piers. But that the builder's intention was neighbourly is made quite clear by the modesty of the façade. The stone is creamy-white with a touch of yellow, enhanced by the green of a magnolia which has been allowed to cover part of it. The tall windows, four of them subtly narrower than the rest, a cornice with dentils below, the doorway and a strongly hipped roof, are almost the only elements in an utterly satisfying design.

Here, then, we have an unspoiled example of a perfect Queen Anne house. Its architect is unknown. Its former attribution to Wren was based on nothing more than its excellence of design, and should be disregarded except as further evidence of his fame and influence.

The interior of the house was furnished and redecorated by its former owner, Mr Denis Martineau, in a manner that does full justice to the outside. Much of the original decoration remained, if by the term 'original' one can marry the 1700 panelling with the 1740 plasterwork and fireplaces which Charles Longueville, a brother-in-law of Charles Mompesson, added at the later date. There are only four rooms on the ground floor of the main house. Between them is a hall which seems full of light even when clouds hang heavy overhead. At the far end of it is a staircase, the most delightful feature of the house. It rises in two flights separated by a half-landing. On the right-hand walls as you ascend, are swags and picture-frames of white plaster against a blue background. The banister-rail is supported on each tread by three exquisitely turned wooden balusters and is finished at the hall end by a sweeping curve as graceful as a curtsy.

Mr Martineau presented Mompesson House to the National Trust in 1952. He was by profession an architect, and every corner of the house and its garden reveals his understanding of the period and his affection for the place. He died in 1975, and the National Trust has since redecorated the main rooms, furnishing them with exquisite pieces loaned or given.

The staircase rises in two flights, and the walls are decorated in white plaster of the eighteenth century.

Powis Castle
Powys

THE CASTLE LIES ON THE BORDER BETWEEN England and Wales, a mile or so on the Welsh side beyond the River Severn. The actual boundary is not the river, as it would have been between two English counties, but the hills to the east of it, emphasizing that this was once a military frontier as well as a civil. You can see the castle quite clearly from the watershed. Steely strips of the river glint from the floor of the intervening valley, and half-way up the wooded slopes on the far side is a dark mass of stone, irregular in outline but large and solid enough to promise substantial fortifications. Seen from this distance, it could be a ruin, like most of the border-castles; but approaching closer, you find that its walls are sound, its windows intact, its park and garden in perfect condition. It is quite clearly a castle which has become a house. Nor is it a nineteenth-century reconstruction. Powis is the greatest house in Wales, not in size necessarily, for there may be others larger, but because it has been added to, patched, adapted, redecorated and embellished with consistent good workmanship from the thirteenth century until the present day. Chronologically Powis could have been placed almost anywhere in this book: it has been allotted to the early eighteenth century because then the garden was given its shape and the castle was rescued from the crisis that could have toppled it into ruin.

It is not difficult to spot the earliest work. On the north and bleakest side (but 'bleak' is here a relative term, for Powis in sunlight is a fairy-tale castle), the fourteenth-century curtain-wall of the Barons de la Pole swings its semi-circular bastions along the edge of a steep ridge, below which was dug a moat. On its inner side the wall helps to form a forecourt, previously the outer bailey. Its entrance portals were built by the third Baron Powis after 1667, but at the far end one is switched back again to the fourteenth century. Two massively rotund towers squeeze between their cheeks an entrance doorway which is lengthened into a corridor by arch upon arch of coiling stone. This entrance is further prolonged into the heart of the house by a narrow courtyard open to the sky, and leads out again on the far side by further gates terminating in a broad flight of stone steps. It is still possible to obtain a good idea of the mediaeval character of Powis by opening all these gates from one end of the castle to the other. One can imagine a friend wending his way on horseback

between the vast stone walls; an enemy left snarling on the threshold of the outer bailey. It was clearly a tough nut to crack, the mansion of a very powerful family.

At every turn one finds evidence of the attempts made by succeeding generations to increase its convenience and comfort. Although the rooms retain their irregular shapes, they have been given classical face-lifts by panelling and larger windows, and in the last quarter of the seventeenth century a staircase of palatial grandeur was added within the north-west corner, leading up to a set of state-rooms that ring the interior courtyard on the first floor. Some of these rooms, like the dining-room on the ground floor, were modernized by G. F. Bodley in the early years of this century, and he chose a mock-Elizabethan style which conforms well enough to the central period of the castle's long history. But the most pleasing rooms are the Long Gallery built by Sir Edward Herbert, who bought the castle in 1587; the State Bedroom, with decorations of the time of Charles II; and the Blue Drawing-room which dates from the early eighteenth century. These three rooms, spread over a century and a half, have been fused by time into a unity of subdued colour, and the whole is further bound together by furniture, tapestry, books and paintings that would not be out of place in any interior except the most modern. To wander through the rooms at Powis is to telescope one's impressions of seven centuries of British civilization. The strong old walls were equal to any modifications within them: a watch-tower became a bathroom, a dungeon a wine-cellar, a guard-chamber was transformed by Chinese wallpaper into a drawing-room, a passageway lifts by short flights of steps over an awkward inner bulkhead, the purpose of which has long been forgotten. From the windows there is a view of fields and woods so soft that they seem touched in by a painter's brush. Even the little town of Welshpool assumes from the distance of a mile the character of a scene from Grimm.

Almost every old house has been the victim of a regrettable lapse. At Powis it was the reconstruction of the windows in the late nineteenth century. The stone of which the castle was built is the ruddy rock on which it rests, almost indistinguishable in colour from Georgian brick. The stone was rough-hewn, giving the walls a pleasantly variegated texture, but when the Elizabethan windows were repaired, the stone was smoothed and cut with a harsh regularity that time has not yet softened. In spite of it, Powis wears as romantic an appearance as any connoisseur of border-castles could desire. Its situation, castellation, circular chimneys, bold rounded projections and irregularly disposed turrets, lift the huge building high over the countryside as if to announce that the Princes of Powis would brook no interference with their patrimony. In later ages, the castle's aloofness was mitigated by the structural changes already described, but most of all by its garden.

Along the south-east front the ridge drops sharply away to a valley. Originally this was merely a boulder-strewn slope with a marsh at its foot, stiffening at intervals into bare walls of rock rising to the platform on which the castle lies. In the late seventeenth century the first Marquess of Powis began the transformation of this slope into six terraces. A print dated 1700 shows that

The south front seen from across the garden. The conical yews were planted in the early eighteenth century. Below them are the terraces which are the most famous feature of the garden.

ABOVE *A view along one of the upper terraces. Lead statues of shepherds and shepherdesses, dating from the eighteenth century, stand on the balustrade.*

LEFT *The Long Gallery built by Sir Edward Herbert, who bought the castle in 1587. The plasterwork ceiling dates from 1592.*

OPPOSITE *The Blue Drawing-room, one of the state rooms which ring the interior courtyard at the level of the first floor. They were extensively redecorated in the early eighteenth century.*

the three upper terraces had been constructed by that date, and well before 1742 the whole scheme was completed by the second Marquess of Powis after his reinstatement. A Dutch water-garden, now a large rectangular lawn, was formed in the valley floor; above it rose the terraces, the back of one forming the platform of the next above it, right up to the castle walls. The four upper terraces survive, but the lower two, which were merely grass walks, have reverted to banks covered by flowering shrubs.

The terraces look their best when seen individually from the level of each in turn. When they are viewed from the mount on the far side of the valley, banked one above the other, the pattern is to some extent blurred, the flowers are indistinguishable and the wonderful view towards the English border is of course lost. The finest viewpoint of all is from the second terrace looking down on the third. A row of urns stands on the balustrade of each, and on the centre of the lower balustrade are four lead statues of shepherds and shepherdesses in Tyrolean attitudes, probably by John Van Nost of Dublin or Henry Cheere, a pupil of Scheemakers. It is extraordinary how these statues steal the show. They are not very large, and there is much else to attract attention. But the vigour and charm of their execution and their perfect siting give the whole auditorium of the terraces a centre-point to which the visitor's eye will turn again and again.

On the east side of the terraces are hedges of yew over thirty feet high, gnarled by age inside but presenting outwardly a fresh apron of yellow-green shoots from top to ground. Further yews have grown from the little soldier-bushes shown in the 1742 print into huge conical trees at the foot of the castle walls. Lower down, the great lawn, flattened in the eighteenth century for the water-garden, now runs like a vast stadium into the curve of the hillside, which is covered by a wilderness of ornamental trees and flowering shrubs. At its eastern end there is a further drop in level to the old kitchen-garden, transformed by the late Lord Powis into a quieter garden of box hedges and short avenues of pyramid apples.

To many people the garden at Powis is its chief attraction. It is of equal interest to the botanist, the student of the history of garden design and the person who only wishes to enjoy a summer's afternoon on its terraces and steps. But castle and garden should be seen together, as a superb use of the opportunities which the lie of the ground presented to the border-barons of the fourteenth century and their more subtle successors in the eighteenth. What the first found sturdily convenient, the second rendered attractive. In their own ways, each succeeded brilliantly.

OPPOSITE *The staircase of Powis Castle, constructed within the mediaeval walls late in the seventeenth century.*

OVERLEAF *The south front of Chatsworth, which was designed for the Duke of Devonshire by William Talman in 1687.*

Chatsworth
Derbyshire

CHATSWORTH IS THE FIRST NAME that comes to mind when one thinks of great English houses. 'Houses like Chatsworth, Blenheim, Hatfield, Knole …' we say, beginning to count the gems in a glittering necklace, but however much the order of the others may vary, it is always Chatsworth first. The reasons for this are various and cumulative, but it might be useful to begin by stating what Chatsworth is not, in order to emphasize later what it is. It is not the largest private house in England; its rooms are not as magnificent as Houghton's or Holkham's, nor is its exterior as great a work-of-art as Kedleston's, Wilton's or Longleat's; it has not been the scene of events as significant in history as those associated with Hatfield or Blenheim; it was not, until the motor-age, very accessible, and one might have expected this to have had some effect upon its fame; and it does not incorporate, at least visibly, the structure of any period earlier than that of William and Mary. That is quite a formidable list of negatives. Yet Chatsworth is still visited by hundreds of thousands of people annually, who rightly feel that to see this house at least once in a lifetime is an essential part of an Englishman's experience. Why?

The answer can be given by an equivalent list of positives. Its situation; its garden; its palatial appearance; its works-of-art; its ducal atmosphere. All these are incomparable. And for those who take the trouble to find it out, there is the strange story of its original construction and subsequent alterations.

A house had stood higher up Chatsworth's hill in the Middle Ages, but its true history begins with Elizabeth Cavendish, 'Bess of Hardwick', who in 1549 persuaded her husband to buy the manor and to erect on it a house even vaster in its main structure than that which we see today. It occupied the same levelled terrace above the River Derwent and contained the same internal courtyard, but it was four, in parts five, storeys high, instead of the present three, and attached to it on the river side were outbuildings proportionate to the state which the Cavendishes kept. No stone of this house can now be seen except by climbing into the roof, but at least one of its inner walls extends into the core of the present house. It was one of several houses where Mary Queen of Scots was kept in decorous confinement during the fifteen years when she was in the custody of the Earl of Shrewsbury, Bess's fourth and final husband. It stood entire for about a hundred and twenty years.

OPPOSITE *The State Drawing-room at Chatsworth. The tapestries were woven at Mortlake in about 1635 after cartoons by Raphael. The ceiling paintings are by Laguerre.*

An aerial view of Chatsworth from the west.
At the foot is the River Derwent, and
descending from the woods is the famous
cascade. To the left of the main house is the
long wing added by the sixth Duke of
Devonshire in the early nineteenth century.

This was the house which the fourth Earl, later the first Duke, of Devonshire inherited in 1684. It was reported to him that the old building was 'decaying and weake', and he determined 'to pull down the same or great part thereof'. We owe the present Chatsworth very largely to him. At first his intention was to rebuild one front only, the south, 'When he had finisht this Part,' recorded his private chaplain after his death, 'he meant to go no farther.' But the building mania of his great-great-grandmother had bitten deep into him, and one reconstruction was followed by another until the whole of her house had been replaced. One must therefore look upon Chatsworth as the product of a single man's energy, working by trial, error and fluctuating enthusiasm and fortune over a total period of twenty years, 1687–1707. As the Elizabethan house was built on a rectangular plan, the Duke was able to rebuild each front separately, shoring up the 'decaying and weake' parts until the new front was far enough advanced to lend them its own support. In speaking of 'new' fronts, one should not imagine simply a face-lift to bring the appearance of the house up to date, but the total destruction and reconstruction of the wing to its full depth and height, except where the old inner walls were sound enough to be made use of. But because two sides of a nearly square house, and all four sides of its interior courtyard, can be viewed simultaneously, no sooner was one finished than the Duke became dissatisfied by the contrast between the old style and the new. Thus he was led, front by front, like changes of scenery on a stage, to rebuild the entire house afresh. His piecemeal methods made necessary architectural devices which can still be seen on close scrutiny, and they were not always very happy. No doubt, if he could have foreseen the end of his work at the beginning, the Duke would have started by pulling down the whole of Bess's house to its foundations and built his own house from scratch. In that case he would certainly have reorganized its arrangement of rooms and entrances and might even have moved the house higher up the hill where it would have been clear of flood-water and dominated the landscape.

The Duke encountered other difficulties of his own making. The first was his inability to visualize the finished appearance of a façade or a room from architectural drawings. Once it was there before him, he would order the destruction of part of it so that it could be rebuilt a second time in a manner more in keeping with his new ideas. The second difficulty was financial. Hanging over him during the early period was a fine of £30,000, awarded against him for the ludicrous offence of tweaking the nose of Colonel Cole-peper, one of his political opponents. The fine was waived in 1689, but for a man who was engaged on building a palace and was heavily addicted to horse-racing in addition, it was a limiting factor on his architectural ambitions. Both failings led to constant quarrels between the Duke and his architect and builders. He could not, or would not, pay the bills. He claimed that his further rebuilding, when he changed his mind on seeing the finished work, was allowed for by the contract, and that the price should remain the same, just as if the contractors had been engaged on the same terms as employees on his estate. A further obstacle was a shortage of coin of the realm: his agents could not supply the necessary amount of loose cash even when the

Duke chose to pay. Clearly he was in a weak position, legally and financially, and the matter was eventually brought to court. Sir Christopher Wren was sent down to Chatsworth to adjudicate on the costs incurred up till 1692, and he assessed them at £9,025.16.6¾, 'with very little or no proffitt to the Archt.', whose reward for his pains was left to the Duke's discretion.

The architect of the south and east wings was William Talman. He was not widely known when the Duke first employed him at Chatsworth, having previously completed only one major building, Thoresby House in Nottinghamshire, of which Hawksmoor later said, 'It was never good, and was burnt down as soon as finished.' After the Duke's squalid quarrel with him, Talman was not invited to submit designs for the other two fronts, and it remains in doubt who was responsible for them. It could have been Thomas Archer, to whom the Duke left £200 in his Will 'in acknowledgement of his favour and his care and trouble touching the building of my house'; it could conceivably have been Wren, who may have sketched a design while he was at Chatsworth; it could have been John Fitch, who signed and approved a version of the west front which is still preserved; or it could have been the Duke himself, by that time fed up with professional men, with the assistance of skilled master-masons in whom he was more successful in inspiring confidence and loyalty. It is to the first Duke – or to the Duke-cum-Archer-cum-Fitch – that we owe the most original external feature of the house, the bow-fronted north façade by which he contrived to mask a difference in plane between the flat wall-surfaces on either side, an awkward inheritance from the Elizabethan building. This was the last of the new works to be completed. In the same year, 1707, the Duke died.

The house was an original and self-contained adaptation of the architectural style current in the reign of William III. 'It stands', wrote Celia Fiennes, when she visited the still uncompleted house in 1797, 'on a little riseing ground from the River Derwent which runs all along the front of the house. . . . Before the gates there is a large Parke and several fine Gardens one without another with gravell walkes and squairs of grass with stone statues in them and in the middle of each Garden is a large fountaine.' Celia Fiennes was not so interested in the façades as she was in the garden and the interior, but her omission makes no difference, since three out of the four stand almost unchanged to this day. They have a noble classicism, which is enlivened by much exterior decoration, but decoration so restrained and well-proportioned that it appears part of the architectural concept of the whole. Of the three, the south front is the plainest, the west the grandest and the north the most original. That they were designed by different hands in different circumstances has not affected the external unity of the house. It was not until the early nineteenth century, when the sixth Duke and Sir Jeffrey Wyatville refaced the east front and added a long wing to the north, that Chatsworth suffered from any incongruity in its appearance from outside.

But the interior was less successful. Let it be admitted, with the reservation that one is here applying the highest possible standards, that the major rooms at Chatsworth are unworthy of it. The private apartments, redecorated by the

The west front, probably designed by Thomas Archer in 1700. In the pediment are the arms of the Devonshire family.

present Duchess, are quite charming. But the state-rooms strain after an effect which only a totally new building, conceived as a whole by a single mind from the very start, could have achieved. Its odd history, so well disguised outside, becomes apparent within. The north entrance hall, previously the kitchen, is an attempt by the fourth Duke in about 1755 to bring the front door into closer relationship with the main staircase: the two are connected by a short length of passage parallel to the inner court, but the arrangement is still rather clumsy. The courtyard itself, which could have been a significant feature of the house, is little more than a well within it, and adds nothing to the outlook and little to the lighting of the four wings. The state-rooms, moreover, are all placed on the top floor, instead of forming a *piano nobile* on the ground or first floor, which Italian, French and English architects, after long experience, had found to be the best place for it. You are therefore obliged to climb a tall and steep staircase to reach them. Even allowing for the wonderful view from the windows, the rooms when you eventually reach them do not make quite the impact intended. The visitor feels that he has seen all this before, better done. The rooms are very grand, of course, and while they could not be expected to be in any sense intimate, since from the earliest days they were primarily showrooms for the family's superb art-collection, they lack charm and even swagger. 'The Great Apartment,' wrote Horace Walpole in 1760, 'is vast but trist. Inlaid woods and floors, and painted Ceilings and unpainted wainscot darken the whole.' Modern eyes may agree with his, particularly if they are unsympathetic to the huge ceiling-paintings by Laguerre and (in one case) Verrio which press down upon the spectator. It is certain that the sixth Duke thought Walpole right. Some of his attempts to improve the rooms were disastrous: his gilded leather on the walls of two of them, for instance, or his substitution of huge plate-glass panels for the original windows which have now happily been replaced. But in one case, he and Wyatville created between them the most attractive room in the public part of the house, the library. Partly it owes its success to the finish and colour of the book-cases and furniture, and to the books themselves; partly to the excellent proportions of the first Duke's anachronistic Long Gallery from which it was formed; but most of all, perhaps, because it looks usable and used, a merit which it shares with the untouched and beautiful chapel. The other state-rooms are so obviously designed for display that one begins to pity George V and Queen Mary, to whom the whole suite was allotted during their visit to Chatsworth in 1915.

The surroundings of the house are as little dull as it is possible to conceive. Its natural situation is a beautiful one, with the river pulled out into straightish lengths immediately below and parallel to the west front of the house, the valley cushioning it on either side. Capability Brown was called in by the fourth Duke, in 1761, but less than usual is due to him, for the early paintings make clear that even in the days of the first Duke, the park, while not so extensive as today, was by no means barren of trees, particularly on the east side. The garden, as we now see it, is in the main the creation of the sixth Duke of Devonshire, Wyatville and Joseph Paxton. The formal *parterres* of the

A bedroom in the upper state rooms, which were used only on the grandest occasions, for instance for the visit to Chatsworth of George V and Queen Mary in 1915.

The chapel, which has remained untouched since it was completed in 1694. The ceiling and wall paintings are by Louis Laguerre, and above the altar is Doubting Thomas by Antonio Verrio.

seventeenth and eighteenth centuries became lawns, and on the upper slopes farthest away from the house, elaborate woodlands, mingled with flowering shrubs, were planted with the utmost forethought. In the middle of these glades one comes across endless surprises – fountains, temples, rustic pavilions, lakes, serpentine hedges, grottoes, and the foundations of the vast conservatory which anticipated Paxton's Crystal Palace. Yet it is none of these things that catches the visitor's eye at first: for within easy sight of the house are two enormous waterworks, the Emperor Fountain and the Great Cascade. The first was contrived by Paxton himself for the sixth Duke in 1843, and its single jet of two hundred and ninety feet is still the second highest, after Geneva's, in Europe. The second is a waterfall of staggering proportions, which dates back to 1696 and impressed Celia Fiennes in the next year almost as much as the water-closets which had been newly installed inside the house.

These are two of Chatsworth's triumphs. But the house itself is the triumph of a man deeply involved in his country's politics, harassed by enmities and debts, who nevertheless managed to find the time and energy to create a masterpiece.

OPPOSITE *The Emperor Fountain, which can send its central jet to a height of 290 feet. It was constructed by Joseph Paxton, the sixth Duke's gardener, who later designed the Crystal Palace in London.*

BELOW *The Great Cascade is a waterfall of staggering proportions, which was first constructed in 1696 and has remained in working order ever since.*

Castle Howard
Yorkshire

THERE IS ROOM TO SPARE IN THIS BROAD SHOULDER of Britain. The fields, like the views, are generous in size. As you approach the area of Castle Howard – and 'area' is the right word to apply, for it is more than a site – you notice that something is happening to the countryside. A sense of expectation is being created, as by the tuning of an orchestra before the curtain rises. The roads become more taut, the farms more regular. The impression is heightened by the silver splinter of a lake, an avenue dead straight for five miles, a column and an obelisk standing stiffly among the trees. From one direction you see suddenly the circular Mausoleum, lonely on its bare hill; from another, a pyramid squatting in the plough; from a third, you pass through curious outworks: a stone gateway, heavily rusticated, with flanking pyramids, battlements and towers; next, to right and left, a curtain-wall broken by turrets, in shape circular, pentagon, octagon or square; then another gateway, with a further pyramid, much larger, sitting over its arch. All this is not immediately intelligible, and was not intended to be. The mixture of motifs and periods – Roman, Egyptian; mediaeval, Tudor – announce the work of a daring innovator and a rich patron, neither of whom was tied by fashion or the fear of ridicule. Then, on the base of the great obelisk, comes hard information. An inscription proclaims the following:

> If to Perfection these plantations rise,
> If they agreeably my heirs surprise,
> This faithful pillar will their age declare
> As long as time these characters shall spare.
> Here then with kind remembrance read his name
> Who for posterity perform'd the same.

> Charles the III Earl of Carlisle
> Of the family of the Howards
> Erected a castle where the old castle of
> Henderskelfe stood, and call'd it Castle-Howard.
> He likewise made the plantations in this park
> And all the out-works, monuments and other
> plantations belonging to the said seat.
> He began these works
> In the year MDCCII

The north or entrance front. The wing on
the right-hand side of the picture,
designed by Sir Thomas Robinson in the
mid-eighteenth century, is wider than
Vanbrugh's opposite wing, and is not
linked to the central block by his curved
colonnade.

The date, curiously enough, is wrong. The first drawings for Castle Howard were made during the last year of the seventeenth century and work began not in 1702, but in 1700. The architect was Sir John Vanbrugh. Space must be found to retell, familiar though it is, the outline of the strange story of his commission. Vanbrugh had never built so much as a garden shed before he embarked upon the design of the greatest private house of its day. He was not an architect at all: he was a soldier turned playwright. But just as he had sat down one day in 1695 to write *The Relapse, or Virtue in Danger*, with no previous knowledge of the theatre, and found himself acclaimed overnight a rival to Congreve, so he was immediately accepted by the young Lord Carlisle as his architect on the strength of a few sketches for a great house which Vanbrugh had roughed out for little more than the fun of it. The sketch, as it happens, was not particularly good, and lacked many of the more striking features, including the dome and outlying courtyards, which were to make Castle Howard the most original building of its age. Nor had Vanbrugh any technical knowledge of how to translate his ideas into stone:

> *Van's genius,* [wrote Swift] *without thought or lecture,*
> *Is hugely turn'd to architecture.*

Three things combined to turn it. Vanbrugh's personality – a friendly, gaily adventurous young captain's manner – which made him a favourite in the Kit Cat circle of Whig landowners and intellectuals of which the Earl of Carlisle was himself one of the most engaging members; the breach between the Earl and the more tetchy William Talman, the architect of Chatsworth until the Duke of Devonshire had found him too difficult to work with (in fairness to Talman it must be repeated that one reason was the Duke's inability to pay the bills); and the friendship which had grown up between Vanbrugh and Nicholas Hawksmoor, Wren's chief assistant.

Seldom can there have been a happier professional relationship than between these three men. Not a hint of jealousy marred their correspondence, and it was all the more remarkable in the case of Vanbrugh and Hawksmoor than of Wren and Vanbrugh. Wren's reputation in 1699 was established unshakeably at the top, while Nicholas Hawksmoor, three years older than Vanbrugh and twenty years a practising architect, might have resented the exchange of a genius for a talented amateur as his master, when he was already proving himself an artist in his own right by his unassisted design for Easton Neston in that very same year.

Vanbrugh handled this delicate situation with great tact. In the words of Laurence Whistler's summing-up, 'Hawksmoor was far from being a mere subordinate. It was he, an excellent draughtsman, who turned Vanbrugh's sketches or rough elevations into working-drawings, and it is possible, and even probable, that a great part of the detail was his own.' Vanbrugh never surrendered to Hawksmoor the credit for Castle Howard, and Hawksmoor did not claim it. Their relationship throughout, as later at Blenheim, was that of senior and junior partner. But Vanbrugh never made a decision without consulting Hawksmoor on its technical feasibility and was careful to explain

The south front. The dome and part of the façade were restored after a fire in 1940.

to Lord Carlisle that this was his practice. To their collaboration one must add one other: that between the two architects and Lord Carlisle himself. Mr George Howard, the present owner of the house, has paid this wholly deserved tribute to his ancestor: 'There are a number of flattering references to his genius, both by George London when speaking of the gardens, and by Hawksmoor himself when writing of work on the house. These often tend to be dismissed as the usual tactful compliments to a patron, but I suspect that they may mean more than that, and that he really was directly responsible for much that has been praised as the work of others.'

The changes that were made in the design as the work progressed have been described in detail by Mr Howard, Laurence Whistler and Kerry Downes. Let us start with the south or the garden front; for although this is not the larger of the two main fronts, it is the more magnificent, the less altered and the more pleasing. A central block is crowned from behind by a high dome and flanked by two one-storey wings, as light as orangeries, supported on a rusticated basement. These are the essentials of the design. We can ignore the slight asymmetry which was due to Sir Thomas Robinson's mid-eighteenth-century 'completion' of Vanbrugh's western wing, for the fact that the two terminal pavilions are quite different in design, and that there is one more window on the west side than on the east, is not immediately apparent. The Corinthian pilasters and the dome take command of the whole façade. Talman had already experimented with external pilasters at Chatsworth a few years before, but here they come in two sizes, huge on the face of the central block, miniature by comparison on the wings. The effect is like a line of guardsmen trooping their regimental colours. One of the secrets of the façades is the alternation of plain surfaces with decoration, and rectangular window-openings in the basement with arches on the main floor. The deep fluting of the pilasters makes a series of vertical stripes which combine with the generally horizontal lines of the building to give it a wonderful balance when viewed from almost any distance. Even without the dome, as can be seen by placing a thumb over it in the photograph, it would still be a building of beautiful proportion, and indeed the dome was one of Vanbrugh's after-thoughts. Remarkably, it enhances an already self-contained façade, and when one remembers that this was the first dome to be designed in England (just after St Paul's and contemporary with Greenwich) and the first on any private house, its maturity and boldness are quite astonishing. It makes no apology for its presence. It is pulled out from the centre of the house on a tall drum like a section of a telescope, and its brilliantly gilded lantern shines out over the park like a beacon. A word of caution and credit should be added here: this is not the original dome, which was totally destroyed by fire in 1940. It is a careful reconstruction by Mr Howard, and he added the gilding on the evidence of paintings in the house which unmistakably show that the original dome was thus enriched.

On the north side of the house is an even more grandiloquent display. Not only do the wings on this side break forward to contain a terraced forecourt; but on each flank there were to have been a kitchen-court on the east and

A corridor within the central part of the house.

stables on the west, fronted by archways and crowned by smaller domes which made them an integral part of the house and trebled its width. The whole scheme can be seen in the etching from *Vitruvius Britannicus*. In fact only the eastern extension was built, and the west side of the entrance court was left uncompleted on the Earl's death in 1738, and was finished by Sir Thomas Robinson in 1759 to a different and wider design. The entrance archways and outer forecourt were likewise never executed. But even the incomplete work is staggering in its originality and size. From a distance it passes every test; it is noble, dramatic, splendid and in scale. From a closer view, there is almost nothing in British architecture to match the explosive vigour of its soaring stone. Only from the middle distance does this front appear to some eyes slightly lacking in cohesion. There is a weakness about the articulation between the main wings and the kitchen court. The low lid-like domes on the four corners of the court sit a little unhappily on their dishes, and less care has been taken with the detailed design and construction of these buildings, probably because they would seldom be seen from within or from outside the house. A further awkwardness in Vanbrugh's original design was well disguised by Robinson fifty years later. The elevation of the west front is now an excellent and unbroken Palladian façade. In Vanbrugh's plan there would have been a deep and rather shapeless indentation behind the south front, as the *Vitruvius* plan makes clear. But here again, had the stable-court been built as planned, the west front would not have been visible as a whole.

Castle Howard is a house on the very largest scale of private building, but apart from the mid-eighteenth-century Long Gallery, its rooms are surprisingly small. There was no suite of state-rooms distinct from the family's quarters. The Carlisles lived in the main rooms along the south front, and the bedrooms were in the west wing and on either side of the Saloon. The reason for this is that the 'orangeries' are in effect only one storey high, and the greater part of the central block is taken up by the huge entrance hall. Comparatively little has been made to go a very long way. This is greatly to the advantage of the house. It does not overawe like Blenheim. It catches up the visitor and retains his affection. The long internal corridors, in which Vanbrugh delighted, consist in arch beyond arch, linked by vaulted ceilings, and create an impression of great distance and coolness. The same is true of the hall itself. Here is architecture on a vast internal scale, but the hall remains astonishingly light, both in the clarity of every part of it and in the lack of any heaviness. This effect is achieved partly by breaking up the two side-walls above the fireplaces by openings into the staircase wells; and partly by the delicate base to the dome, from which angels should be blowing trumpets. Standing immediately beneath its central point, one looks up into the recently repainted underside of the dome, and cannot imagine a more successful or more daring combination of strong uprights and circular bands.

The photographs must be allowed to speak for the ornamentation of the park and gardens. Each of these beautiful stone buildings was placed in its present position with the utmost forethought for the effect which it would create from the windows of the house and the terraces. It would be difficult to

The Satyr Gate, designed by Vanbrugh as one of the entrances to the walled garden.

The Mausoleum designed by Nicholas Hawksmoor, Vanbrugh's collaborator at Castle Howard. It stands on a bare hill half a mile east of the castle.

choose between Vanbrugh's Temple of the Four Winds, Garrett's bridge over the river and Hawksmoor's Mausoleum. Each in its own way is a masterpiece of delicacy contrived from heavy blocks of stone. The Mausoleum is a building of very great originality, both inside and out, and removes any lingering doubt whether Hawksmoor was an architect of the first order. The Temple destroys at one stroke the legend that Vanbrugh was incapable of gracefulness, while the bridge, which leads merely from one field into another and never had a road across it, is a reflection of classical design with which even the Palladians could find little fault; Garrett indeed, was a protégé of Lord Burlington.

These buildings are the most important in a whole group which surround Castle Howard to a distance of a mile or more. The modern visitor to the house leaves it with an enduring impression that the minds of several great men have met here to create what is without question the finest memorial to the short-lived age of the English baroque.

Antony House
Cornwall

SOME HOUSES, LIKE SOME PEOPLE, are immediately likeable: others take time to know. Antony belongs to the first category, and its charm remains as fresh to those who have spent a lifetime in it as to the visitor of a single day. The impact which it makes is as instantaneous as that of an exceptionally pretty woman seen suddenly across a crowded room. That the eye can distinguish the minute variations of feature which make the difference between a pleasing and an unpleasing face, a pleasing or unpleasing façade, is one of the more enjoyable of human faculties. One calls it 'a sense of proportion', and although that does not explain all, one can be persuaded when confronted by Antony to believe that a science of aesthetics must really exist. Antony could be dissected element by element, but if such an analysis could answer the question How?, it can never quite answer the question Why? Why does it give us such delight? Why does one know that so long as men enjoy beautiful things, a house like this will be recognized as a perfect example of its kind? And there is another question. Why is Antony so unmistakably English? After all, it shares with every famous old house on the continents of Europe and America the same classical ancestry. Its tall windows are by origin French, its pediment Greek, its door-frames Italian, its dormers Dutch. But it is sited, put together, composed in a manner that justified the English boast that for short snatches of time, one of which was the late seventeenth and early eighteenth centuries, loosely called 'Queen Anne', we achieved an indigenous style of architecture that has no rival in the world.

Antony was built by an unknown architect between 1711 and 1721 for Sir William Carew, whose family had lived for centuries in an older house nearby, the exact site of which has been forgotten. It is deceptively simple in appearance. Its two main façades, north and south, like the two side-elevations, are identical. Nine windows extend along the first storey, eight below, with a doorway under the central window, and six dormer windows set into the hipped roof above. The chimney-stacks are plain up-ended boxes spaced unapologetically at equal intervals against the skyline. The surface decoration is reduced to a minimum. There was no true porch on either side (the present *porte-cochère* at the entrance front is an addition of about 1840), but merely a simple grouping of shallow pilasters and a cornice to frame the doorway. The central bay projects by no more than twelve inches. The angles of the house are slightly emphasized by rusticated quoins, there is a string-course marking the floor-level of the first storey, a strong plain pediment above the door and smaller pediments above the dormers. That is all. The secret of Antony's dignity and welcoming appearance lies in the spacing of these different elements, and in the silvery colour of its slate roof and Pentewan stone. Even the small square panes of its white sash-windows are an essential part of the design, for they add a touch of intimacy, a diminution of scale at precisely the right point, promising warmth and hospitality within, without in any way minimizing its fine appearance from outside.

If one wished to give a lesson in the principles of proportion, there could be no better way than by comparing the reality of Antony with the painting overleaf by a local artist soon after its completion. It is recognizably the same house, but an error of drawing has fractionally increased the height of the building and reduced the scale of its windows so that nobility has become mere elegance. Alternatively, take the Borlase etching, which shows the true proportions, and cover up the pediment or eliminate for a moment the angle quoins, and you have something which the least sensitive observer will immediately know to be incomplete, even if he could not explain why. Antony is indeed struck true and firm from its die.

The central block or pile (but both words are too gross to describe a temple dedicated to domestic bliss) could stand in any company on its own – in a cathedral close, for example, or in eighteenth-century Piccadilly. But because this is the country, the architect could afford the space to enclose the forecourt by two wings which frame the house and add to its variety. He did so with exceptional daring. Within the general Wren context of the building, the wings are treated quite differently from the main house. The material is brick, not stone. There is much greater freedom of movement in the two colonnades, which anticipate by their tall arches the motif which we shall find constantly repeated inside the house. On the four corners of the court are set spiked cupolas which add a note – the only note – of frivolity, entirely successful in the case of the front pair, but they are seated a little uneasily on the corners nearest to the house, where one would have preferred a repetition of the two front pavilions by continuing the colonnade through to the garden instead of closing the vistas by a wall. Above the central part of each colonnade rises a second storey, a laundry on the left, a kitchen on the right. Originally there was also a row of dormers in each roof – they can be seen in both early drawings here reproduced – and the roof itself was flattened at the top to avoid any competition between the wings and the house. A low wall closes the fourth side of the courtyard. The combination of the brick wall and stone piers binds together the different elements of the composition most attractively. The circular drive within the courtyard, the statue (now replaced by a sundial) at its centre, cupolas as light as meringues to right and left, the curved iron gates and the twenty arches on either side, give the front entrance exactly the spring and colour needed to accentuate the pale simplicity of the façade.

One expects to find the interior equally light and graceful. There will be

plaster swags on the walls and ceilings, perhaps a delicate circular staircase and fireplaces of restrained elaboration. The great windows must surely fill the rooms with sunlight and open them up to the superb view of which one has already caught a glimpse from the drive. This is true of the first floor, where charming bedrooms lead off a central corridor framed by tall open arches continuing down its length. But the ground floor was conceived quite differently. With the country so immediately available, the emphasis is on coolness and seclusion within. The rooms are small and intimate, facing north and panelled in dark Dutch oak. Only one, and that the smallest, has windows in more than one wall. All of them are arranged round a central hall with an eye to convenience and privacy more than for effect. The staircase rises from the hall in two broad flights, the turned balusters, three to a step, compensating for its rather heavy construction. Here again one finds tall arches dividing the outer from the inner hall, which give the interior movement – the only characteristic that it has in common with the contemporary conceptions of Vanbrugh and Hawksmoor.

For all these reasons the rooms at Antony probably look their best at night. They require, and have been given, low lighting, wood fires and heavy curtains. The excellent series of family portraits (some of the best are by the young Reynolds, who was born not many miles away) and the fine furniture, porcelain and books appear to perfection in this subdued atmosphere. Antony is a house to be lived in, wholly and continuously: it needs bustle, flowers, comfort and affection.

One further aspect of Antony needs to be described, its setting. The house stands half-way down a long slope leading at about a mile's distance to one of the many estuaries which ultimately combine to form Plymouth Sound. The wooded combes, half-sea, half-river, on the borders of Cornwall and Devon were ready-made for the landscape painter, and even more for the landscape gardener. Capability Brown had no hand here, but even in its natural state it could have inspired his unique contribution to the English scene. West of the house are hedges of clipped yew, tall, dark and widely spaced. Eastward lie farm buildings which share something of the serenity of the house. But to the north the view is open to the gently falling valley, with glimpses of water and farmlands beyond.

'Rich the robe, and ample let it flow,' quoted Humphrey Repton ecstatically when he was called in to advise Reginald Pole-Carew at the end of the eighteenth century. 'It is worth considering', he added in a pencilled note to his employer, 'how far future generations may be benefited by a disgusting eyesore [of new plantations] for the present.' Happily they chose to sacrifice present amenity to future glory. Clumps of trees were planted, vistas cut through the woods and the rigid lines of earlier avenues and stone walls were swept away. Today Antony – the very name reflects its masculine grace – is cushioned in firm hills and lies palely beautiful against a background of meadows and trees.

*The hall, from which the staircase ascends
beyond the two archways.*

NICHOLAS HAWKSMOOR BUILT FROM SCRATCH and his own invention only one country-house, and it was Easton Neston. It was not completed as he intended it, perhaps fortunately, for the wings and entrance-screen that he later proposed to add were imitative of Vanbrugh, and among the many virtues of the house is that it stands in time as a very individual creation, and in space as a breathtakingly pale and self-contained building which any additions would have spoilt. Hawksmoor himself would not have shared this opinion. He as deeply regretted that his full design was never executed as Vanbrugh despaired of Lord Carlisle's loss of interest in building the stable-block at Castle Howard. No doubt if we could see in stone the full array of Easton Neston as Campbell illustrated it in *Vitruvius Britannicus*, we would not wish to part with any of it. But it would not have made the same impression. Walking through the park to the point where Hawksmoor optimistically built his entrance-piers, one looks back to see the south front of the Petit Trianon miraculously translated to Northamptonshire. It anticipated Gabriel's little masterpiece by over fifty years. But everything that has ever been said in praise of the Trianon applies equally here. There is the same creaminess of stone, the same lift of the Corinthian pilasters, the tall windows, the rusticated basement, an almost identical balustrade on the flattened roof, and, most significant of all, the same proportions. Easton Neston has been called an example of the short-lived English baroque, and so it would have been if the full design had been carried out. But in its present imperfectly perfect state it foretells the full flowering of the eighteenth century in the century's first years. Externally it was finished in 1702.

Hawksmoor, said Sir Reginald Blomfield, 'was incessantly trying to translate Vanbrugh in terms of Wren'. As Hawksmoor was Wren's master-draughtsman at Greenwich and St Paul's and Vanbrugh's junior partner at both Castle Howard and Blenheim, it made a neat and damning summary of a great man's work. Even Laurence Whistler quoted it with approval in his biography of Vanbrugh. But with Easton Neston at the beginning of Hawksmoor's independent career and the Castle Howard Mausoleum at the end of it, this judgement cannot be allowed to stand. The commission to build Easton Neston for Sir William Fermor, Lord Lempster, fell into Hawksmoor's

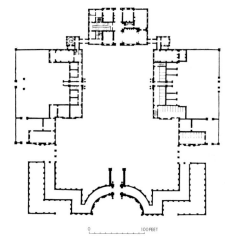

The original plan of Easton Neston shows Wren's wing on the left, and the stable-block on the right, which was built, but demolished in the late eighteenth century. The elaborate forecourt was never constructed apart from the entrance-piers at the foot.

The entrance front looking towards the Wren wing on the north side. The two wings were probably designed by Wren in about 1680, but the main building, begun in 1696, was entirely the work of Hawksmoor.

lap at exactly the moment when his artistry could profit from it most, for Wren's influence on him was beginning to fade and he had not yet met Vanbrugh. By 1696 Wren had picked out Hawksmoor from among his young pupils as the one whom he could most readily trust with original and unaided work, and he recommended him to Lord Lempster to complete the house on which Wren himself had advised some fifteen years before. Two wings of 'Wren's' building (the inverted commas are necessary because it is unlikely that Wren even visited the site, and he probably did little more than sketch a design to please his relation-by-marriage) faced each other across an empty forecourt, and one of them survives. It is a decent brick building with stone facings to the doors and windows, one-storey high externally, with dormers so mean that it seems probable that they were inserted later. Hawksmoor himself described the wings, in an untypically disloyal phrase, as 'good for nothing'. Such forthright condemnation was undeserved, but there is no doubt that the building which Hawksmoor erected between them completely overshadows the earlier work in scale and quality.

It is not known how Wren would have completed the building, if indeed he ever drew out the full design. In about 1682 – the letter is dated by the month only, and not the year – he wrote to Sir William that he hoped the house would soon be making progress, and added, 'I will, if I can, set it out.' Probably it would have been a stone-faced building not unlike Stoke Edith or Antony. But for reasons that can now only be guessed, the central block was never built by Wren. The wings stood isolated for years on top of a gentle rise, like the wings of Mellerstain before Robert Adam, and Sir William Fermor continued to live in the Tudor house of his ancestors a short way down the southern slope. Shortage of money is the most likely explanation of the delay, for in 1692, the same year in which he was created Lord Lempster, Sir William married an heiress as his third wife and his architectural ambitions then revived significantly. He took Wren's advice to call in Nicholas Hawksmoor, and the building was under construction by 1696 or 1697.

No written documents have yet come to light to illustrate the evolution of Hawksmoor's ideas or the relations between him and his patron. But something even more dramatic has survived: Hawksmoor's original oak model. This chunky doll's house, which stands in a corridor at Easton Neston, takes to pieces. The entire roof lifts off, and below it there are little lids, like those on breakfast-dishes, that can be removed to expose various rooms, and the whole first-floor section slides out to reveal the ground-floor plan. Internally the model shows the house almost exactly as it was built. But externally, between the model-stage and the actual building, changes were made to the two main façades which greatly enhanced their originality and appearance. The model carries in the centre of both entrance and garden fronts a double row of superimposed orders – rusticated pillars on the garden side and engaged Corinthian columns on the entrance side, the latter reminding one irresistibly of the main temple façade at Petra. In execution Hawksmoor made three alterations: the building was slightly heightened and narrowed; the double columns became pairs of pillars or pilasters rising almost the entire height of

the house; and between the windows and at the corners he repeated the pilasters round all four sides.

The effect is quite astonishing. It is a palace in miniature. The first impression, in much more than the hygienic sense, is of its cleanliness. The Helmdon stone is the finest of all English building stones, for it is unmottled and unveined, as clear as liquid, but where it is rounded, as in the two vast columns on either side of the front door, it acquires a certain swarthiness, like a lion's pelt. It can be carved with a crispness which more than two hundred and fifty years of weathering have not dulled, and the Corinthian capitals, the only one of the classic orders that can turn a corner effectively, are as sharp as freshly cut acanthus leaves. Hawksmoor matched the elegance of his material by an arrangement of doors, windows, external staircases and subtle recessions that clothe the glowing skin of the façades with the minimum of fuss or ostentation. Not a rainwater pipe is allowed to mar the composition of the main fronts, and when the pattern of windows and pilasters is varied, it is by curvature so simple that it does not destroy the overall effect.

The park is Hawksmoor's, with its canal on the axis of the garden door; but the view in the other direction was Wren's, or Wren's deputy's, for the house was sited frontally to face at two miles' distance the lonely spire of Greens Norton church, one of the few instances where the late seventeenth century acknowledged the existence of any period of English civilization previous to its own. The garden, however, is modern, the creation of Lord Hesketh, who died in 1944. A paved terrace, set with yew toadstools and snail-like patterns in box, overlooks a pool surrounded by roses and terms grinning from a hedge. On a June day, when the accompanying photographs were taken, the controlled fecundity of this garden, its gently stirring water that always seems to overflow but never does, the abandon of the roses and formal curves of yew, form a bower that is scarcely a lesser work of art than the house itself.

The golden light is let in to all the rooms of the house. Not only are the main windows almost as high as the ceilings, but Hawksmoor contrived through the centre of both floors a long gallery that opens them to the views on each side. He has been gently chided by Kerry Downes, his biographer, for 'treating the interior like a box, giving it a number of large stately rooms, and filling up all the remaining spaces with as many small rooms as possible'. But what is any house but a set of boxes within an outer casket, and if the casket be noble, what does it matter that the boxes be of different shapes and sizes and differently orientated, provided that each is a delight in itself?

The rooms at Easton Neston pass this test without fault. Partly it is due, of course, to fine furnishing, pictures, chandeliers and tapestries, but also to Hawksmoor's original conception, evident in the model stripped to its ground floor, that rooms must vary in shape as they vary in purpose, and that their arrangement must hold in reserve some surprises. His staircase, which rises in a long flight that turns back on itself to complete the slow climb to the first-floor gallery, imposes on the house a certain stateliness of rhythm. But the rooms themselves do not suffer from any excess of grandeur.

The one heavily decorated room, the drawing-room, was the work of a local plasterer in the mid-eighteenth century who let himself go in a riot of picture-surrounds and a ceiling in high relief that would have shocked Hawksmoor, a man uncommonly lacking in humour, but has delighted its occupants ever since. The present appearance of the dining-room, too, would cause Hawksmoor to throw up his hands in despair, for it has been formed from the lower half of the central section of his Great Hall. The change, made in the late nineteenth century, was undoubtedly the right one, for Hawksmoor's hall, with its bare upper walls and lower 'vestibules' on each side, was one of his few unsuccessful innovations. But to end on a note of criticism of this great architect is quite inappropriate to a description of a house which gives the visitor such intense pleasure. Easton Neston is without equal for its grace, its sunlit dignity and its architectural audacity that transcends the mere piling of stone on stone.

A corner of the drawing-room. The elaborate plasterwork was added after the room had been completed by Hawksmoor.

Blenheim
Palace
Oxfordshire

THE FASHION FOR REWARDING NATIONAL HEROES with great houses has passed, but the next best thing is to be born in one, as Winston Churchill was born at Blenheim in 1874. A hundred and seventy years earlier his ancestor, John Churchill, first Duke of Marlborough, had defeated Louis XIV's Marshal Tallard at the Danubian village of Blindheim or Blenheim, and the people received him on his return to London with an ecstasy that recalled the rejoicings after the defeat of the Spanish Armada. Queen Anne took the lead in proposing that the most suitable mark of her and the nation's favour would be a house, castle or palace (Blenheim has been called all three, but later generations have settled for 'palace', the only one in England that is not royal or episcopal), and as a site she gave the Duke her manor of Woodstock.

The Duke was invited to choose his own architect. He chose Vanbrugh. The choice was not the natural one, for Sir Christopher Wren was Surveyor of the Queen's Works, and Vanbrugh, his junior in age and rank, was still known only as the architect of Castle Howard and the author of some amusing plays. The Duchess of Marlborough pressed Wren's claims for this pearl of a commission, and one might have expected the Duke to capitulate from distrust of his own judgement and a wish to please her, But he showed unexpected vision. Wren would have designed a lovely brick palace like his great addition to Hampton Court or his unexecuted rebuilding of Whitehall — very neat, very gentlemanly, very English. But Vanbrugh alone had the capacity to translate a Roman triumph into stone.

He and the Duke met at Woodstock in February 1705, only six months after the Battle of Blenheim. They selected as the site for the palace an elevated platform on the side of the Glyme valley opposite the mediaeval manor. The foundations were being dug by June of the same year, and by 1707 the east wing was ready for its roof. Few buildings can have been begun under happier auspices. Marlborough and Vanbrugh each recognized in the other the highest qualities of their respective professions; Queen Anne was more than delighted with the design; Vanbrugh had persuaded Hawksmoor to help him with the detailed execution of the work; Marlborough continued to win victories. Only one person was not pleased: the Duchess.

If ever there was a woman bent on mischief, it was Sarah Jennings, Duchess

The entrance front looking across the
Great Court.

of Marlborough. She conceived for Vanbrugh a loathing from which nothing would deflect her. Her vindictiveness stemmed from the rejection of Wren, but it soon became clear that she and Vanbrugh had totally different conceptions of what Blenheim should be. She wanted a comfortable country-house. He saw it as a building in which convenience and elegance should take second and third places to monumentality. She was worried about the cost of his grandiose designs, for she wisely foresaw that the royal favour might not always shine so brightly and that the Marlboroughs might have to pay. He regarded the commission much as Le Nôtre might have regarded Louis XIV's, as a licence to spend whatever was necessary to achieve the most glorious effect. The basic incompatibility in their points of view led to quarrelling so bitter that it is a wonder that the palace was ever finished at all.

The scale of Blenheim was very large. Much more was made of the two side courts, which had entrance towers and façades of much greater regularity than those of Castle Howard, and these courts were withdrawn from the sides of the main house to give it an east and west front as well as a north and south. Perhaps Vanbrugh was dissatisfied by the way in which the service-courts at Castle Howard obscured the sides of the house and were articulated to it, and there is no doubt that the side-elevations of Blenheim are more satisfactory. On the other hand, many people will prefer the two main fronts of Castle Howard. There is nothing at Blenheim so immediately engaging as the dome over the central building of Castle Howard. Instead, we have a columned portico which appears slightly too high for its width, topped by a curiously chunky affair of stubby pillars and broken arches above the pediment. To the right and left there is a curved porch, again heavily surmounted by a rectilinear second storey behind it, and at all four corners a great tower of deliberately outlandish design. Then begin the Tuscan colonnades. The whole façade is angular, massive, stern. All the obvious aids to elegance have been rejected. Even the decorative features are intentionally bizarre, like the finials to the towers, a duke's coronet perpetually burning in the flames of a grenade. Robert Adam, who admired Vanbrugh more than any of his predecessors, felt compelled to comment, 'His taste kept no pace with his genius, and his works are so crowded with barbarisms and absurdities, and so borne down by their own preposterous weight, that none but the discerning can separate their merits from the defects.' The Great Court at Blenheim, like the garden front at Holkham, has left 'the discerning' at loggerheads. Horace Walpole could call it 'a quarry of stone'. Voltaire remarked 'que c'était une grosse masse de pierre, sans agrément et sans goût'. But Sir John Soane wrote, 'This work alone may be said to stamp Vanbrugh the Shakespeare of architects'; and Sacheverell Sitwell, that it is 'one of the most extraordinary feats of architecture'. That the finished result should continue to arouse controversy would no doubt have pleased Vanbrugh. He did not set out to delight, nor even to shock. He was constructing the back-drop to a Wagnerian opera. The heaviness of the stone, the thick duplication of the central part, the massed battalions of columns, make the building intensely dramatic and challenging. It is like a declaration of war.

OPPOSITE *The superb west front of Blenheim Palace. In the foreground is the formal garden created for the 9th Duke of Marlborough by his French architect, Duchêne, in the early years of the present century.*

OVERLEAF LEFT *The hall at Castle Howard, looking downwards from the staircase. It is 52 feet square and rises to a dome 70 feet high. It is one of the most impressive conceptions in English architecture, to which a sense of spaciousness is given by the arched openings on all sides.*

OVERLEAF RIGHT *The garden front of Easton Neston seen from across the ornamental pond. The main living rooms look out over the garden, which was made in the 1920s.*

The south or garden front seen from the lawn, originally a formal parterre.

OPPOSITE *The architectural grandeur of Blenheim is reflected by many of the doorways which separate the various state rooms.*

Moving round to the garden fronts, you find something of much more immediate appeal. It is true that the military symbolism is maintained by a huge bust of Louis XIV, a trophy from Tournai mounted centrally above the south portico, the eighteenth-century equivalent to exposing the severed heads of your enemies on your gates. But on this side Vanbrugh's treatment of the huge masses was quieter and more conventional. On the two side-fronts he allowed himself a certain grace of movement, now greatly enhanced by the formal gardens laid out by the ninth Duke and his French architect Duchêne in the early years of the present century.

The same consideration had its effect upon the design of the inside. Vanbrugh has often been accused of sacrificing his interiors to the exteriors, of condemning his patrons to live in draughty halls and move with guttering candles through endless corridors. But the criticism cannot be sustained by the same person who finds Vanbrugh's rooms small and mean. The truth is

that Blenheim and Castle Howard were both designed for a way of life that no longer has much meaning for our own generation. There had to be an entrance of overwhelming magnificence and a reception room equal to the dignity of the privileged few who were likely to be invited there: hence the Great Hall and the Saloon, the first painted by Thornhill, the second by Laguerre. But there must also be intimate rooms for the family, where the scale was reduced to closets where conversation could burgeon and one would not be too overawed to lay down a pipe. Blenheim is not often praised for its interior, apart from the icy blue emptiness of Hawksmoor's Long Library, perhaps the finest room he ever designed. But to dismiss the rest as un-memorable is to do Vanbrugh less than justice. You find, to your surprise, that a habitable house has been built within a temple.

Vanbrugh is equally to be credited with his forethought for the surroundings, which provide an English setting for the baroque palace without bringing one into conflict with the other. His vast *parterre* on the south front has been swept away, but round the other three sides he transformed the royal hunting forest into a park of dimensions appropriate to the scale of his architecture and as green as baize. The vast bridge, which became the biggest bone of contention between him and the Duchess, lacks its superstructure, and from the house appears little more than a causeway across a deep valley. But walk to one side and you will see at once that this 'wasteful' edifice is in fact a master-stroke. It was to be 'the finest bridge in Europe'. Wren had prescribed something far less pretentious, but Vanbrugh's persuasiveness and sense of the magnificent won the day. There it stands, Appian in its stupendous bulk, and, like the palace, a symbol of triumph. He made only one mistake: in his day it crossed a slender canal, and it was left to Capability Brown to form the lakes on either side which gave the bridge something worthy to surmount.

ABOVE *The Long Library was intended by Vanbrugh as a picture gallery, but was finished by Hawksmoor to house the Sunderland Library, which was sold in 1872. The fine stucco ceiling is by Isaac Mansfield.*

OPPOSITE *The Great Hall rises to a height of 67 feet. The combination of huge Corinthian columns and high arched openings is typical of Vanbrugh's style.*

223

Mereworth
Castle
Kent

THE HOUSE WHICH COLEN CAMPBELL DESIGNED at Mereworth for John
Fane, later seventh Earl of Westmorland, in 1720–3 was a close copy of the
Rotonda, or Villa Capra, which Palladio had built in the mid-sixteenth
century for Paolo Almerico, a town official of Vicenza. This capsule of
concentrated information can be swallowed whole or dissected, and dissection
appears the better course, for why a Scottish architect who had never been to
Italy should choose to erect an Italian villa in the Weald of Kent for a patron
who had likewise never set eyes on the Rotonda, demands some explanation.

The story should begin with Andrea Palladio himself. He achieved in
England a reputation that surprises Italians even to this day. His work was
derivative from earlier Renaissance buildings which themselves derived from
Imperial Rome, and by his time the style had been almost exhausted of its
possibilities. But his famous volumes *I quattro libri dell' architettura*, first published in Venice in 1570, had been Inigo Jones' bible and were republished in
an English translation by Nicholas Dubois in 1715 with plates specially
redrawn by Giacomo Leoni. Among the illustrations were an elevation, a
cross-section and a ground-plan of the Rotonda, probably the most famous of
the many villas which Palladio erected in the Venetian plain. Undoubtedly
Campbell, the originator of the English Palladian style, worked from these
drawings when he came to design Mereworth. As Palladio was Jones' idol, so
was each of them Campbell's. He admired but rejected Hawksmoor and
Vanbrugh in favour of what Summerson calls 'the search for absolutes', that
purity of style which the Romans originated and Palladio followed. Of course
Mereworth was not an exact copy of the Rotonda any more than Palladio built
exactly as the Romans did. Both made concessions to contemporary tastes and
comforts. The Rotonda was a Roman temple in form more than a Roman villa;
and Mereworth is an English Palladian house more than an Italian *villegiat-
tura* resort. Nevertheless the artistic descent from Rome to Kent is direct.

Colen Campbell, in the third volume of his *Vitruvius Britannicus* (1725), drew
attention to the changes which he had made in translating the villa from
Vicenza to the neighbourhood of Maidstone. 'I shall not pretend to say', he
wrote, 'that I have made any improvements in this plan from that of Palladio
for Signor Almerica, but shall only observe the alterations which I humbly

The castle from the south-west, illustrating the
basic composition of a rectangular block with
classical porticoes on all four sides, and
surmounted by a dome. On the right is one of
the two pavilions which were added in
1736–40, about fifteen years after the main
house was completed.

submit to my learned Judges.' These alterations were significant. Mereworth lies towards the bottom of a wide shallow valley and until the late nineteenth century was surrounded by a moat; the Rotonda stood on a tumulus. Mereworth has an outside staircase on two sides only, the north and south; the Rotonda on all four sides. Mereworth has a smooth outer dome of lead; the Rotonda's was layered and tiled. Mereworth's twenty-four chimneys are ingeniously fed through the shell of the dome into a single chimney at the top, disguised as a lantern; the Rotonda's chimneys emerge as obelisks on the outer walls. In the Rotonda the porticoes have arches at the sides; at Mereworth the sides are columned. Inside, Campbell also departed from his pattern by retaining only one of Palladio's four vestibules that linked the porticoes with the central hall and so managed to fit in a drawing-room extending the unbroken length of the south front. 'And if I may add', concluded Campbell, 'the great difference both of dress and materials, the whole ornamental parts being of Portland stone.'

All this amounts to quite a difference, and judges, learned or not, are likely to admit that each change was an improvement. Still, Mereworth remains an imitation and a tribute. Other houses were built in England after the same model, notably Lord Burlington's villa at Chiswick and, at one stage removed, Lord Herbert's in Whitehall and Stourhead, Wiltshire, but Mereworth is the most faithful to the original. Nobody would have built like this unless compelled by admiration for a shape. It is a symmetrical shape that manages to achieve great variety. Here is a square two-storeyed block surmounted by a dome with an identical pedimented portico on each side. Those are the essentials of a composition visible from every direction. Yet the wonder of Mereworth is that you can walk round its outside without monotony. This is due not only to the change in the fall of light and shadow – and Mereworth must for this reason be seen in sunlight – but to the continually changing spatial relationship between porticoes and house. Each step backwards or forwards alters the relative position of the columns, as can never happen when mere pilasters are flattened against a formal façade. Portico is seen in relation to portico, at least two at a time, and when the house is viewed frontally, three. All of them are beautiful combinations of stateliness and ornamentation. Their ceilings are of great richness, but they are only discovered from within, like those of the Parthenon peristyle, and the eye is constantly choosing between the decoration of these porticoes and their plainness. The dome, of course, is unchanging from every direction, and its ornament is its structure – prominent ribs and a lidded cupola. The latter at first seems to need glass panels at the sides (which it cannot have, because it also does duty as a chimney) or failing glass, gilt, on the analogy of Castle Howard's. But on second thoughts one comes to agree that Mereworth is not a house that should glitter: the glitter is inside. It is a house of profiles and silver stone.

Campbell makes no reference in his book to the two exquisite pavilions that stand one on each side of the entrance front, and it now seems certain that they were not built until about 1736–40, about fifteen years after the main house was finished, and perhaps by 'Athenian' Stuart. Not only are they

Looking across from the portico of the west pavilion to its pair opposite.

pretty buildings in themselves but they are perfectly sited in relation to the house, close enough to frame it but not too close to cramp it nor to interfere with the dignity of the stepped approach. Had it not been for the porticoes and the moat, the architect might have followed the Palladian tradition of linking the pavilions to the house by curved and colonnaded wings, and we can count ourselves fortunate that this mannerism was not possible here. It was also a happy notion to place arcaded loggias on the sides of the pavilions that face the house and porticoes on their inner fronts, so that the rhythms of the house are maintained but not repeated, and extra views from and towards the house are created. Although the moat is lost, Mereworth still seems to swim. It is a very light structure. The dome might be gas-filled, anchored by its square base to the ground.

Every chance passer-by must want to go inside. For how, he asks himself, can people live in such a place? Is there a room within the dome? And what happens at the angles where straight walls meet curved? The answers, in their order, are as follows: that they live very comfortably; that the dome forms a hall in the form of a half-egg, rising from floor level to the base of the cupola, with a gallery ringing it at the level of the first floor; that spiral staircases fill two of the corners, a lift the third, and a small cloakroom the fourth. The structure and ground-plan are very ingenious. But not even the best photograph can convey the total impression made by the lovely circular hall in the centre of the house. Campbell called it a Saloon, but it is doubtful whether it could ever have been used as a living-room since its only windows are the circular recesses at the base of the dome, and it is a place where furniture is superfluous. The inside walls are painted in terracotta, slightly roughened in imitation of the colour and texture of the walls of an Italian villa. Against it lies the white stucco of Bagutti. This takes the form of swags of flowers and fruit, allegorical figures and boys reclining above the doorways, busts on wall-pedestals or cupped in shells, enriched soffits to the gallery, plaques, friezes and pilasters. Thus catalogued, the stucco may sound overdone. The photograph proves that it is not. The circular shape makes possible the continuity of the pattern without a break, and the height – who does not first look upwards when entering a domed hall?– lifts the eye away from the drum below. Horace Walpole, who visited Mereworth with John Chute in 1752, called the hall 'a dark well'. Even making allowances for his bad temper at the time, of which his letters give ample proof, no judgement could be more ridiculous. But of the rest of the house he had more good to say. 'I must own', he concluded, 'that it has recovered me a little from the Gothic.' From Walpole that was high praise.

The other downstairs rooms are richer than the hall. The doors and doorways are as sumptuous as Holkham's, and not a square inch of the coved ceilings is unadorned by paint or gilt except where they were left unfinished. They are none the less extremely habitable rooms. Partly this is because they are inhabited – humanized by the comfortable clutter of a family's daily life; and partly because the colours, though rich, are fused to the gentle tones of tapestries. The long drawing-room is so immediately attractive that the visitor finds himself guilty of looking around it before greeting his hostess; while the

The base of the circular hall which lies beneath the central dome. The elaborate stucco decorations by Bagutti are contemporary with the building of the house.

smaller rooms vary between ornamental closets and state-rooms that can still be used to sleep, eat, write, play billiards and even bath in without feeling that one is doing these things in surroundings that demand a special behaviour. The climb upstairs by the spiral staircase to the gallery affords a unique pleasure: until the last moment you are hidden from the renewed surprise of looking down on the hall from the base of the dome.

Mereworth is a house of paradoxes. By following after a fashion the antique rules of temple architecture, it breaks the rules of house-planning. A villa in descent, it is a castle by name. A house that could be freakish in its Kentish context, is immediately recognizable as a great work of art. Rooms that belong to a palace never overawe. Mereworth is a remarkable incident in the long flirtation between Italy and the Gothic North.

The Drawing Room which runs the full length of the south front.

Ditchley Park
Oxfordshire

IMAGINE AN ENGLISH PARK IN SPRINGTIME, where beech-leaves as crisp as lettuce drip over a lake and fields are spotted yellow with cowslips or brown with recumbent cattle, and place in the middle of it a great grey house. The eighteenth century tailored the surrounding countryside into shapes which still cushion the house and provide walks and views for its occupants. It is romantic but always under control. The winding water is dammed by a firmly ruled dyke, and the great woods are lanced by rides or 'lights' which terminate in a circular temple or, on clear days, the distant towers of Oxford. The eighteenth century abominated a view that was unbounded.

Against this background, and raised above it on a platform, lies the house. It is in three linked parts, a massive pile joined by curving colonnades to a substantial wing on each side. The wings, one originally intended for the kitchen and laundry, and the other for horses (but it also contained a chapel), are externally more charming than the main house, which is sober to the point of starkness. It starts well, with two superimposed rows of tall windows, but it ends abruptly, as if the original plan had never been completed. The roof-line is clearly wrong; the statues (of Fame and Fortune) are placed too close together, and the chimneys look like materials dumped for further building that was never carried out. A last-minute economy may have been the reason. A drawing for Ditchley by James Gibbs, its architect, shows a pediment and two cupolas like those designed by William Kent for Badminton, and in another Gibbs version, a temple frontage of columns, either of which would have pulled the design together in the manner that strict classical proportion demanded. In a third drawing two further statues are shown on the parapet which would have made the existing couple seem less lonely.

Something of this sort must have been intended, since the two wings are, in contrast, perfect in their symmetry, their hipped roofs sloping to platforms for two balanced clock-towers which form exclamation-marks each side of the solemn centre-piece. These wings are exceptionally pretty. Stand one of them in a modest garden visible from the road, and no traveller could fail to draw up with a gasp of pleasure. Part of their attractiveness, as of the whole house, is the weathering of the Burford stone, grey spotted with ochre, and a silvery lining to the cornices.

One of the two exquisite wings which are linked to the main house by curving colonnades on each side.

The entrance front, which appears not to have been completed precisely as James Gibbs designed it in the 1720s. The top storey seems more truncated than classical proportion demands.

The house was built by Gibbs in the early 1720s for George Henry Lee, the second Earl of Lichfield, grandson of Charles II and his lovely mistress Barbara Villiers, Duchess of Cleveland. It replaced the Lees' Elizabethan house which lay a short distance away, and some of the materials from the old house were used in the construction of the new. Ditchley has changed little since then, and has been marvellously preserved because it had the good fortune to fall into the hands of poor men when taste was bad, and rich men when taste was good. What contents it has lost have been well replaced, and most of its decoration was in any case irremovable if not indestructible – moulded cornices, elaborate door- and window-frames, marble fireplaces, niches, statuary, bas-reliefs and splendid family portraits built into the walls. It is a perfect example of a high, but not the highest, degree of ostentation thought suitable for a nobleman in the early eighteenth century.

The ground floor was composed of nine rooms (now eight, because a dividing wall was demolished to form the present library) arranged round a central hall, which alone rises through the second storey. The two staircases are modest, ingeniously tucked away to avoid any interruption to the circuit of the state-rooms. You pass through splendid mahogany doors, often doubled, to rooms of different sizes, each a surprise for its varying decoration. Only the hall is enormous. It is approached direct from the outside steps, and forms a vast cool cube in the centre of the house, which could be, and has been, used as a main drawing-room, but was primarily intended as a place for movement and greeting, and to set a tone of scholarship and refinement immediately on entry. Sculptured figures representing the arts and sciences recline in pairs over the three main features of the hall (a fireplace, an alcove opposite it, and the doorway leading into the Saloon) and busts of eminent writers and philosophers stand on brackets high on the intervening walls. A large oval painting by William Kent fills the centre of the ceiling. It is one of the loveliest rooms in Britain, the heavy style of the period being wholly appropriate to its scale. The more delicate filigree of fifty years later would have trivialized its monumental calm.

The most charming of the other rooms is the White Drawing-room. Here is found a rare later importation, an 'Adam' ceiling which suits it well, for although the room is a strong one, with two superb white and gilt eagle-tables by William Kent, and a voluptuous Lely of Barbara Villiers facing his portrait of her royal lover down the length of the room, it is at the same time coolly decorous, its dominant colour being ivory laced with faded gold.

Beyond the Blue Parlour is another surprise of the house, the Saloon. Here William Kent, who with Henry Flitcroft took over most of the decoration when Gibbs had finished the structure, employed three Italian stuccoists whom he brought back from his continental tour, and gave them free rein to embellish walls and ceiling with plaster decoration in high and low relief, mostly of classical figures depicted in Baroque draperies and attitudes of graceful abandon. Nobody who has once seen Ditchley could ever again accuse the early eighteenth century of dull conformity to established taste. The house is a triumph internally, a triumph of scale, of variety of materials, and of a peacefulness induced by the subtlest use of strong elements.

Ditchley passed collaterally to the Dillon family some twenty years after it was built, and remained in their hands until shortly after the death of the seventeenth Viscount Dillon in 1932, when it was providentially bought by Ronald Tree, a Member of Parliament. He and his wife Nancy relieved the house of the accumulated clutter of the previous century and modernized it extensively, for when they acquired it, it had no heating, no electricity and only one bathroom. He also restored the park and garden to the condition that Capability Brown had intended in 1770, forming the grass terrace, three hundred feet long, at the foot of the garden front. It became one of the loveliest and most comfortable country-houses in Britain, and one of the most hospitable. Winston Churchill, who had visited Ditchley once in the 1930s, was a self-invited guest when Chequers was under threat of air attack, and used it as his headquarters during thirteen week-ends between 1940 and 1942. It was there that he first heard of the landing of Rudolf Hess in Scotland, and there

Looking from the hall into the Saloon. The hall is pre-eminently the work of William Kent, who placed above each doorway reclining figures representing the arts and sciences.

LEFT *The Saloon, which was decorated under the direction of James Gibbs by three Italian stuccoists. The antlers are a hundred years older than the room, and are trophies of hunts in the reign of James I.*

OPPOSITE *Ditchley Park seen in springtime from the garden side.*

OVERLEAF LEFT *The Saloon at Kedleston. The ceiling is formed by the dome which is the central feature of the south front. The decorations and furniture were designed by Robert Adam, down to the very locks on the doors.*

OVERLEAF RIGHT *The Saloon at Saltram, one of the largest and most beautiful rooms that Robert Adam created.*

that he worked out with Roosevelt's emissaries the details of Lend–Lease.

The latest transformation of Ditchley is the most remarkable. No country-house in modern times could be put to more appropriate use. It was bought in the 1950s by David Wills, and presented by him (before he had spent a single night there as its owner) to the Ditchley Foundation, a non-official organization which arranges conferences for senior executives in Britain, the United States and other countries. In these beautiful rooms they spend unadvertised week-ends discussing political, economic and social policies of common interest. It was not a use of Ditchley that James Gibbs or Lord Lichfield could possibly have foreseen, fortunately, for then they would have planned it differently. But a great country-house serves today as admirably for a meeting of minds as it did for the gatherings of family and friends during the previous two hundred and fifty years.

Holkham Hall
Norfolk

ABOVE THE INNER SIDE OF THE FRONT DOOR at Holkham is an inscription more modest in its proportions than in its claims. 'This seat,' it reads, 'on an open barren estate, was planned, planted, built, decorated and inhabited the middle of the XVIIIth century by Thos. Coke, Earl of Leicester.' A pedant could object that not all these statements are quite true. The estate, far from being barren when Lord Leicester inherited it at the age of ten, was rolling sheep-country and had supported for over a century a large and distinguished family who lived not more than a few hundred yards from the present house. He had the controlling hand over the design and execution of his new building, but he was assisted by friends and professionals even more knowledgeable than himself, and by an army of skilled craftsmen. He did not live in more than a corner of it, because he died five years before its completion. But such carping criticism would be out of place at Holkham. Lord Leicester should be allowed his note of triumph. By inspiring the idea of Holkham, by seeing it through twenty-five years of its construction (1734–59) and filling it with the books and works of art that he had collected in his youth, he was the author of one of the greatest memorials to the Palladian age.

Holkham makes an immediate and overwhelming impression of stateliness; but it also strains the critical powers to the utmost. For its exterior is not, in the facile sense, attractive. It is built of a yellowish brick, as near a copy of the Roman Renaissance brick as the Norfolk kilns could manage, and its south elevation lacks that liveliness and balance which one has come to associate with the prettier achievements of Palladianism. Its relieving features are the great portico, the Wilton-like caps to the corner towers of the main block and the triple-pedimented façades to the wings. That is all. The eye searches for pleasing colour, and finds it only in the great red curtains of the central windows; it searches for the more obvious signs of grace and movement, and finds them in the arches of a large orangery and the curve of a garden balustrade, only to recoil with something like guilt from these Victorian additions. The windows flanking the portico appear lost in the expanse of brickwork above them, and the basement windows are as plain as portholes.

The question which then forms in our minds is why the incomparable trio who created Holkham – the Earls of Leicester and Burlington, and William

OPPOSITE *The Marble Hall at Holkham, which rises to almost the full height of the house and was modelled by William Kent on the design of a Roman basilica. The great columns are of Derbyshire alabaster.*

The south front, a carefully designed adaptation of the Palladian style. It is 344 feet long from wing to wing. On the right is the large Victorian orangery.

Kent – adopted this austere external manner. It is not convincing to dismiss it as ugly or a mistake, nor to suppose that they were incapable of more 'stylish' architecture. The south front goes beyond mere elegance. It is an attempt to sum up in brick the ideals of an age: stoic rejection of frivolity in the essentials of a man's character and conduct, secular robustness and common sense. The placing of the windows was partly dictated by interior design: there are great voids behind those blank walls which were left empty to accommodate high ceilings and the reverse sides of the internal apses. But if a second storey had been thought necessary to the façade, it could have been contrived. Its omission was deliberate. If the house at first appears as functional as a Prussian riding-school, contemplation of the relationship between its different components convinces one that here is an organization of masses and planes which has few equals in the country.

Lord Leicester, we are told by his executive architect, Matthew Brettingham, was insistent on 'commodiousness' throughout his house, by which he meant comfort, ease of access and excellence of construction. Over two hundred years later his care is still apparent. To our eyes there are certain deficiencies, such as the great distances between the kitchen-wing and the

The Long Library, which runs the full length of the south-west wing. It contains the collection of books acquired by the first Earl of Leicester on his Italian tour.

dining-room, and the comparative poverty of the servants' quarters which made it necessary for footmen to sleep four to a bed (not unusual in the eighteenth century) and for the maids' rooms to be split up into attic-cubicles as late as the 1930s. But of the soundness of construction there can be no doubt at all. The craftsmanship of the ceiling and other decorations was worthy of their designers. Almost nothing has had to be changed or repaired since the 1750s. The gilding of the cornices, the doors and window-frames, the carpets and wall-hangings, are the originals. Only in a few rooms has even the paint been refreshed in modern times. At Holkham, therefore, one sees a house of the utmost distinction, exactly as its creator desired it and his widow completed it.

Here is a Roman palace reinterpreted by the English eighteenth century. Its astonishing maturity, its restrained voluptuousness, its coolness, grandeur and disdain of the tawdry, leave no room for doubt that centuries of experiment and artistic creation have led up to this point. It comes as a shock to realize that almost nothing about Holkham except its site can be called basically English. In the official account of the house, published shortly after its completion, every part of it was attributed to its Roman or Italian prototype, or to Jonesian derivations from them. Yet nothing could be less plagiaristic. To take the outstanding example of the entrance hall, the idea of which was credited by Brettingham to Lord Leicester himself. In essence it is a Roman basilica with an *exedra*, surrounded by Ionic columns. But the splendour and grace of this vast hall lies in the device of mounting the peristyle on a podium the depth of the basement floor, and in making the columns out of Derbyshire alabaster, a material which is used again in the facings of the podium and gives the hall its only colour apart from the stair-carpet. It is not in the least like a temple, though it owes its origins to temple architecture. As Arthur Young observed, it is more like a bath-house of the utmost magnificence.

In the rooms that compose the state-suite on the first floor, there is the same absence of fuss. The materials, like the furniture, sculpture and pictures, are of the highest quality, but they are used with such chastity (the word is James Lees-Milne's) that it was possible to decorate the smaller private rooms in the same style without oppressing them. The Long Library in the south-west wing is one example. It is Kent's untouched work, a beautiful room which owes its subdued colour to the calf bindings of Lord Leicester's editions of the classics and to wall-gilding which only becomes apparent as each part is examined in turn. The sculpture gallery, a favourite eighteenth-century room, is one of the few in existence which seems habitable as well as a perfect setting for marble statues. The dining-room expresses perhaps best of all the ideal of classical purity to which the eighteenth century aspired but so seldom attained in their private lives. Though it must often have been the scene of revelry and debauch, it could surely also stimulate a high level of conversation, just as the cricket-ground between the north front and the lake makes a hero out of every village Bradman.

That such a house should have descended to the greatest agricultural reformer of his day, 'Coke of Norfolk', first Earl of Leicester by the second creation, may seem anticlimactic, but only if one pictures an aristocratic yokel clumping up and down these rich rooms. He was not in the least like that. As he pretended to no knowledge of the arts, he had the good sense not to Adamize or Gothicize his great-uncle's legacy during the sixty years of his ownership. 'I shall never venture to interfere with the result of years of thought and study in Italy,' he said, and Holkham could not be better described.

The north dining-room which takes the form of a cube, with a central apse for the serving table.

Saltram
Devon

IT IS A PRIVILEGE TO RISE at Saltram early on a May morning and wander into the garden before the house is opened to the public. The shutters have been folded back, but the blinds are still drawn to protect the fabrics of the great eastern rooms from direct sunlight. There is already a great deal of bustle about the place. The post and milk are being delivered at the back door, gardeners are busy with barrowloads of tonsuring tools, builders and decorators are restoring the eighteenth-century Gothic chapel, and from inside the house comes the hum of apparatus for cleaning and scouring it, and the smell of cooking breakfasts. A great house is wakening to life as it has every morning for over two hundred years.

About eighty people, working full-time or part-time, are employed to service and protect the house. Ten families live comfortably in flats constructed in different corners of it, leaving fifteen of the more important rooms, from the Saloon to the Great Kitchen, open to paying visitors every day of the week from spring to autumn. Nor does Saltram hibernate. At intervals throughout the winter it is the scene of candle-lit concerts (the Saloon is still without electric light), and the work of maintenance and repair goes on unceasingly. One by one the shabby or derelict parts of the house and its outbuildings have been brought to a perfection unknown since they were originally built, and perhaps unknown even then, for rooms and furniture of this quality can be too new. At Saltram the eighteenth century has reached its maturity, like the park and garden which surround it.

What has it lost by passing from the ownership of the Parker family to that of the National Trust, and by opening its doors to all comers instead of to invited guests alone? It would be bold to answer, Nothing. Yet, almost nothing. A great Adam room actually gains from the absence of the family. A pile of old copies of *Country Life* on a rosewood table can hide it unattractively, and a toy train on an Axminster carpet is as incongruous as an inkpot left on a settee. A bedroom is lovelier for being neat, and a forgotten toothbrush in such surroundings is more discordant than endearing, for this furniture was intended to remain as pristine as when it arrived from the cabinet-maker, or to hold objects worthy of it. The state-rooms were in a sense always 'public' rooms. They were used only on the grandest occasions, and were left uncluttered. We are told that when tables were needed for the dining-room, they were carried in, and after the meal carried out, to leave it almost bare of furniture except that which was built-in or placed round the walls. In the eighteenth century the Parkers spent their normal days in smaller rooms like the library and the Morning Room, and these are still habitable in the modern sense, with sturdier furniture and less-expensive carpets, while the more delicate ornaments, now as then, are placed out of reach.

The National Trust have achieved at Saltram the ideal balance between privacy and display. Ropes to prevent straying, mats to save wear and tear, notices to guide and warn, have been reduced to a minimum, and where they are necessary, they are designed in a style that does not violate a room's integrity. The supports for the looped rope in the dining-room, for example, are copies of the carved and painted legs of Adam's sideboard. Moreover, research has identified and explained buildings, pictures and other works of art of which even the later Parkers had forgotten the origins. At no period has Saltram been better understood and cared for than it is today, and in that sense it has never been better loved.

All that it has suffered, through no fault of the Trust's, is the destruction of part of its landscape. Saltram owed its original charm to the proximity of Plymouth; it has lost some of it for the same reason. When the Parkers first bought the property in 1712, the view from the house was south-west across the estuary of the Plym to the spires and fortifications of the city, and the wooded slopes of Mount Edgcumbe beyond. The tidal waters formed a natural lake, and you could enjoy the added diversion of watching sailing ships moving across it. Great woods were planted on neighbouring hills to frame the view, and slowly a woodland garden was formed along the broad peninsula on which the house stands. Several paintings by William Tomkins (1730–92) are preserved at Saltram to illustrate the enchanting combination of these natural and man-made features.

The slow expansion of Plymouth has destroyed much of this. The tidal creek was drained in 1806 to form a race-course, now abandoned to the municipal rubbish-tip, as part of a plan to raise its level before landscaping. Council estates crawled up the hills, and a motorway was carved from their reverse slopes. Pylons straddled the middle distance. A cement works was built within full view of the house, and near it a generating station, which in mist might be mistaken for a castle and cathedral respectively, but in clear light reveal all too brutally their industrial purpose. A strip of wood carefully sited two hundred years ago on the skyline has been reduced by quarrying to a few tattered trees. The only defence against such inharmonious development is to reverse the process, to exclude the views which the eighteenth century opened up. The house has been shielded by new plantings, and when they have grown thick and high, it will turn inwards to its superb garden of tall trees and flowering shrubs, and to the small buildings which adorn it, some classical, some Gothic, like the Orangery, the 'Castle', the chapel, and a little temple known as 'Fanny's Bower' after Frances Burney who spent a happy day there in 1789, looking across the then untarnished estuary.

The garden front of the house is its most attractive, incorporating the original seventeenth-century block between the two wings which were added about fifty years later.

The house which rises towards one end of the ridge seems at first sight unimaginative. Although it is appropriately painted peach-colour, it seems almost bleak, 'extraordinarily undistinguished for its size', as John Cornforth has written, and it is difficult to analyse exactly why, for its elements are clean and classical, and there is much variety in the treatment of three of its four sides (the fourth is a jumble of service buildings). But it is too four-square, too keep-like, too stubborn, its entrance front conventional, and it has a certain deliberate austerity, for instance in the lack of any exterior mouldings to the windows, which are cut as if from plywood, like Holkham's, as simple oblongs to admit light. In the centre of the garden front there is something more pleasing, a decent house built by Sir George Carteret soon after the Restoration, which remains externally almost unaltered though totally transformed within. The eighteenth-century house is related to it quite ingeniously by two low wings terminating in pedimented tower-blocks on each side.

The Carteret house was not the first. A Tudor mansion of considerable size is still in part preserved behind it, later enfolded on three sides by the Parker house. It is one of the joys of Saltram to come across these brick and stone relics of an earlier age and to find embedded in so exquisite an interior three cobbled courtyards surrounded by puzzling masonry of slate sandwiched between brick and granite, with arched doorways, rugged stone fireplaces, a tower four-storeys high on which was later perched a Georgian cupola (long since removed), and labels over some of the inner windows which date the original house at least as early as 1520.

The most distinguished owner of the Tudor house was Sir James Bagg, Vice-Admiral of Devon and Cornwall. One can imagine him on his tower-top with a spy-glass, surveying his ships at anchor in Plymouth Sound. His son paid for his loyalty to the King in the Civil War, and was obliged to sell the house to Carteret. In 1712 it was sold again, to the Parkers (later Lords Boringdon and Earls of Morley), who had lived for nearly two centuries at Boringdon, a few miles away.

The present house is due to the wealth and imagination of two members of the Parker family, mother and son. The mother was Lady Catherine Poulett, a daughter of Queen Anne's Secretary of State, who married John Parker, the son of the purchaser of the estate. It was she who undertook the extension of the house to make it the largest in Devon and Cornwall. She wrapped round the remains of the Tudor house, and prolonged the Carteret house, by new wings which turned Saltram into something totally different from either. She appears to have been her own architect, since no other is mentioned in the surviving records, and there are certain errors of architectural grammar (for instance the columns of the staircase hall) of which a professional would never have been guilty. Her strength of will is as evident in the masculine exterior as it is in the portrait of her by Thomas Hudson in the entrance hall. Inside the house she allowed it more grace and freedom. Many of her interiors survive intact, and the rich stucco ceilings, some of which may have been executed by Italians, and the excellent woodwork and chimneypieces, are evidence of her care for detail and nice judgement of proportion. Her rooms, like the hall, are

Lady Catherine Parker, a portrait by Thomas Hudson. In the 1740s she converted the small manor house into the largest private house in Devon.

The Morning Room, hung with pictures in the crowded eighteenth-century manner. Five of them are portraits of the Parker family by Sir Joshua Reynolds.

low cool rooms, the bedrooms and smaller sitting-rooms perfect of their kind. Four of them she hung with Chinese wallpaper, one of which is thought to be among the earliest papers from the Far East extant in the British Isles. Lady Catherine was described by a contemporary as 'a proud and wilful woman', but she was a true innovator, a true artist. If she cannot quite match for originality and daring one of the other women architects whose work is described in this book, Bess of Hardwick, she was more than equal to the second, Lady Wilbraham of Weston Park.

Lady Catherine died in 1758, eight years after the house was completed. Her son, John Parker, inherited Saltram from his father in 1768, and immediately began the alterations which give the house its major distinction. He employed Robert Adam to construct within the east wing a room, the Saloon, which has no equal in the West Country and few elsewhere. Ten years later, Parker re-employed Adam to convert his library into a dining-room. Saltram is now generally known as an Adam house, such is the dominance of his contribution to it, but only two rooms, and adaptations to a third, are due to him, together with one or two of the garden buildings and lodges.

The Saloon is approached through the Velvet Drawing-room, an immensely rich ante-chamber lined in red Genoa velvet. Two columns at the far end frame the double doors which open into the Saloon. Adam must have enriched this room as a suitable mental preparation for what follows. We know, for example, that the mirrors on each side of the doors were made to his design, and it is tempting to attribute to him the columns too, which resemble, in style and purpose, those in the ante-room at Syon.

It does not always follow that the spirit lifts when the ceiling lifts, but in Saltram's Saloon both do. The room is a double cube of great size, fifty feet long by twenty-five feet high and wide, slightly smaller than Wilton's, but it may have been suggested by it, since John Parker is known to have visited Lord Pembroke's house. You instinctively look upwards on entering it, and see a coved ceiling richly ornamented with Adam's graceful geometric designs, incorporating griffons and lunettes painted by Antonio Zucchi, set like bosses in mediaeval roofs, but infinitely refined. The walls are covered with pale-blue damask hung with pictures, including one of Thomas Parker by Sir Joshua Reynolds, a close friend of Parker and a frequent visitor to Saltram (the house contains ten of his paintings).

The centre of the room has been cleared of all furniture not essential to it, just as Adam intended, so that the rich Axminster carpet forms a main element in its decoration. There are eighteen Chippendale armchairs of the same colour as the walls, and two great settees covered in the same material. They lie each side of a lovely fireplace which incorporates a carved frieze and columns of Sienna marble, and facing it is a Venetian window freed of the stained glass with which the Victorians encrusted it. Other touches of subdued colour are added in other materials – the mahogany doors with gilt-brass handles to them, the gilding of the picture-frames, the Pembroke satinwood tables, two excellent nineteenth-century chandeliers, and four great wall-mirrors designed by Adam himself. The room represents the summit of

England's fine and applied arts. Rich as it is, it creates an impression of gossamer simplicity. Adam exercised a control over his many collaborators to produce a harmonious scheme which is clearly the work of many hands but of one brilliant mind.

Next to the Saloon is Adam's dining-room. He had originally made a library in this space and adapted it ten years later, in 1780, when a more convenient kitchen was constructed nearby after a fire. It is little more than half the height of the Saloon and less formal, the far wall curved to a central

The Great Kitchen, which was completed in 1779, and remained in use until the present century.

window flanked by two arched niches containing Etruscan urns. The colour of the walls is green, and their main decorations are paintings framed simply in white, which like the ceiling, carpet and chimneypiece, were probably part of the decoration of the library. So ingeniously has the adaptation been made that few visitors could conceive that this room ever served any other purpose than a dining-room. Adam designed the furniture to fit it, and by making works of art out of necessities, like the curved sideboard fitted into the window bay, he suffused the room with utilitarian grace.

Lady Catherine Parker brought few pieces of furniture to Saltram from Boringdon, her earlier home, and today it is filled with what she acquired in the mid-eighteenth century, and more importantly with what her son contributed a generation later with the advice of his friends Robert Adam and Sir Joshua Reynolds. Since then, little has been added and little taken away. In 1809 Lady Boringdon wrote of Saltram with the ecstasy of a young bride: 'The place is a thousand times more delightful than all the possibility of my imagination had conceived it. It is so gay, so *riant*, so comfortable and so everything that it ought to be, that it is impossible to love and admire it enough.' 'So everything that it ought to be' could be our own verdict today.

Syon House
Middlesex

SYON IS THE LAST OF THE GREAT PATRICIAN HOUSES around London to remain in the hands of its original owners. The rest have been institutionalized or preserved in the aspic of State ownership. The house is still occupied for several months in the year by the Duke of Northumberland and his family, but its closeness to the metropolis, which swirls round its park on three sides (the fourth is mercifully edged by the River Thames with Kew Gardens on the opposite bank), and the apparatus of guard-ropes and drugget carpets necessary to protect the rooms from prying fingers and stiletto heels, diminish its seclusion and turn some of the most charming rooms to be seen anywhere in England into corridors for tired feet.

The visitor who is ignorant of its contents is not likely to be enticed to Syon by its appearance from outside. Outwardly it resembles an arsenal more than a house. A square battlemented block of brown stone with angle-turrets, its garden front surmounted by a great lion, suggests a Wyatt house more than something basically Tudor. Yet it is Tudor to its bones. The house was raised in about 1550 by Edward Seymour, Duke of Somerset, Protector of the Realm during the reign of the boy-king Edward VI, who made use of the walls of an earlier Bridgettine nunnery that had stood on the site since 1431.

The early history of Syon is an appalling succession of disasters. The house drew to itself people at the crisis of their lives, and passed from one failing hand to another with a rapidity that suggests a curse upon it. The nuns were ejected by Henry VIII in 1534 on a trumped-up charge that their relationships with the friars were more than cordial: one of the priests was quartered, drawn and hanged, in that gruesome order. Henry VIII confined his Queen, Catherine Howard, at Syon during the months before her execution, and his own corpse was mauled by dogs as it lay there in state on its way from London to Windsor. Protector Somerset himself was beheaded in 1552 before the new house was completed, and he was followed to the block by his successors at Syon, Lady Jane Grey, her husband and father-in-law, who had forced the Crown upon her for a reign that lasted no more than nine days. Henry Percy, the ninth Earl of Northumberland, was fraudulently implicated in the Gunpowder Plot, and imprisoned in the Tower of London for fifteen years because he could not pay the £30,000 fine imposed upon him. Syon was for a time the

The garden front. Syon retains the four-square plan and original walls of the Tudor house built about 1550. The lion came from Northumberland House at Charing Cross, demolished in 1874.

prison chosen by Parliament for the children of Charles I. It came in the late seventeenth century to the three-year-old Elizabeth Percy, who was married at twelve, widowed in the same year, remarried at fourteen to Thomas Thynne of Longleat who was almost immediately assassinated in Pall Mall by the order of a disappointed rival, and married for the third time at the age of fifteen to the Duke of Somerset. From that moment Syon at last found peace. It is strange that a house with such a history should have survived at all. It is even stranger that it should contain the finest expression of the imagination of Robert Adam.

In 1760 Adam had not long returned from a tour of Italy, his mind filled with the possibilities of recreating the Roman style in terms of eighteenth-century refinement. He was on friendly terms with the Duke of Northumberland, for whom he helped to redecorate Alnwick Castle, and straight from Alnwick was commissioned to refashion Syon 'in the antique style'. Adam was delighted with the commission. 'I endeavoured to render it a noble and elegant habitation,' he wrote, looking back with satisfaction on his work, 'not unworthy of a proprietor who possessed not only wealth to execute a great design, but skill to judge of its merit.' But Adam was not allowed to do all that he wanted. He was instructed to preserve the original Jacobean layout of the rooms, one running into the next around the four sides of the first floor, and he was not permitted to build over the central courtyard the large circular room, capped by a cupola, from which he intended that all the outer rooms should radiate. He finished only five of the rooms, occupying two-and-a-half sides of the building, but they remain exactly as he designed them, laid out like five playing-cards round the courtyard.

Adam complained that his difficulties were increased by the fact that the entrance hall, probably the old refectory hall of the monastery, was on a lower level than the other rooms. Yet this difference of level imparted variety to an otherwise rather bleak hall, for he was able to introduce steps at each end, increasing the 'movement' of the design, and arousing expectation of what might lie beyond. To some eyes the hall is nevertheless the least successful of the rooms, for its walls and ceilings are unrelieved by colour and the antique statues make it seem cold rather than cool. It is the only one of the five which looks better in a photograph than in reality.

The Ante-Room, approached by the short flight of steps on the right of the hall, is by contrast one of the richest and noblest rooms that Adam ever created. It is quite small, but an effect of Roman splendour is achieved by the twelve columns of verdantique dredged from the bed of the Tiber and brought to Syon in 1765. What a discovery, and how splendidly Adam turned it to advantage! The columns are ranged round the room against the walls except on one side where they are brought forward to give it the semblance of a square, and standing on the Ionic capitals are statues of dull gold which look downwards from just short of the ceiling. The whole room, for which the word 'gorgeous' is for once not inappropriate, is Adam at his most adventurous. Gone is the 'lace and embroidery ... Adam's filigree', at which Horace Walpole unfairly mocked, and in its place is bold design, architecture carried

The Long Gallery, adapted by Robert Adam
from the original Jacobean gallery, and with
furniture specially designed by him. The
grouping of the pilasters, the central placing of
the fireplace, and the design of the ceiling give
the gallery an appearance of greater width.

ABOVE The east doorway of the Red
Drawing-room. The doors were doubled in
order to prevent the smell of food and smoke
penetrating from the dining-room.

indoors, mingled with an unashamed use of strong colours. The floor of yellow, red and blue scagliola work, the ceiling and the gilt stucco wall-panels in the form of trophies, combine to make the Ante-Room a triumph of grandeur on the scale of a private house. It was never a living-room, but was used as a waiting-room for servants – those pipers and Swiss porters whom Walpole observed with a shrug of the shoulders as evidence that the Northumberlands 'live by the etiquette of the old peerage', and were likely to end in financial ruin.

Turning the corner of the house, one enters the dining-room, a treble-cube room sixty-three feet long by twenty-one feet wide and high. Four statues in niches face the windows, the whole finished in gilt and ivory, almost clinically, for Adam believed that dining-rooms in England were places where men liked to linger over their meals talking politics, 'more detached from the society of the ladies' than was the custom in France. So there must be no wall-hangings, not even curtains to the windows, which could retain the smell of food and smoke. For the same reason, the drawing-room must be a sort of insulation chamber to protect the ladies in the Long Gallery from the sound of revelry in the dining-room. The Red Drawing-room, so called from the lovely red Spitalsfield silk which covers its walls, is in fact a great deal more than an air-lock. It is a beautiful room with a coved ceiling painted by Angelica Kauffman in round paper medallions set in gilded octagons, and a carpet, the finest of its sort in existence, woven by Thomas Moore from Adam's designs in 1769. On the fireplace and the doorways (the latter doubled for the sake of his much-cosseted ladies) Adam lavished his most exquisite filigree, a form of classical rococo. The long narrow panels of ormolu on a background of ivory are the perfect expression of that 'variety and gracefulness' which he considered essential ingredients of a gentleman's house.

The fifth and last Adam room is the most astonishing and satisfying of all. Here is the eighteenth-century solution to the residual problem of the Jacobean Long Gallery. The room is one hundred and thirty-six feet long, with a width and height of only fourteen feet, and eleven windows ranged along one side. How was Adam to adapt it 'for the reception of company before dinner or for the ladies to retire to after it'? He finished it, he wrote, 'in a style to afford great variety and amusement'. The three doors and two fireplaces, the bookshelves and highly ornate ceiling expand its apparent width, while groups of pilasters give it extra height. The furniture, all of Adam's design, helps to break up the great length of the gallery. But the first and lasting impression is of its colour, a very pale green enriched with gilt like a potpourri of lavender and faded rose-petals.

Looking back on these five rooms one is conscious of their variety and inventiveness. One is led from the highly enriched classicism of the entrance rooms, which anticipate the style of the French Empire by a generation, to the restful, habitable dignity of the Long Gallery. Syon is a supreme example of the art of decoration. But as Adam said, 'a proper arrangement and relief of apartments are branches of architecture'. Syon is one of those houses which only truly begin at the front door.

Kedleston
Derbyshire

ONE OF THE FEW FORMS OF SELF-DISCIPLINE which great men of the mid-eighteenth century imposed on themselves was a willingness to undergo discomfort and ugliness for the sake of a finished result that they might never live to see. There was a perfectly good house at Kedleston in 1758 when Sir Nathaniel Curzon, later Lord Scarsdale, decided to rebuild it completely on the same site. It was not more than seventy years old. But all had to be pulled down in the interests of fashion and architectural adventure, and for years Sir Nathaniel can seldom have been out of earshot of hammering and shouted instructions. The park was cut up by the transport of huge loads of building materials, a whole village had to be removed because it lay too close to the house, and the turnpike road was diverted by special Act of Parliament.

Sir Nathaniel showed equal courage in his choice, and change, of architects. Kedleston is the product of three men, not working in collaboration but replacing each other as the building progressed and as their patron considered their powers of invention exhausted. The idea of a Palladian mansion connected by curving arcades to four detached wings or pavilions was conceived by Matthew Brettingham, who had been the executive architect of Holkham under Kent and Lord Burlington. It was he who built the north-east, or family, wing at Kedleston in 1758, which allowed Sir Nathaniel to pull down the Restoration house before the work advanced further. Then James Paine was called in to complete the whole building in a more magnificent style, and to him we owe the north front. He was the most distinguished architect of his day, and it needed determination on the part of Sir Nathaniel and a dignified withdrawal by Paine, before Robert Adam could replace him in 1760 without any apparent friction between the three of them. Kedleston is known today as an Adam house, one of the first and major works of his career, and he endowed it with all its originality and most of its distinction, inside and out. But in taking over other men's work he altered little of what they had completed, and both Brettingham and Paine should have some share in the credit.

This double change of architect might have had a disastrous effect on the appearance of Kedleston. In fact, it lost nothing by it. This was partly because each of the three was working in the same general neo-classical context; and partly because it was possible to treat the north and south fronts quite

The north or entrance front, designed by James Paine. On the right is the tower of the parish church. It is all that survives of the village which was swept away by Sir Nathaniel Curzon to make room for his house.

The south front, the work of Robert Adam. Two further wings were to have been added on this side of the house, but they were never constructed.

differently, as neither would be visible in juxtaposition to the other. A third reason is that Kedleston lies in the middle of a rolling park so lovely that almost any stone building of the appropriate size would be enhanced by it. The plan, however, was not quite completed. For reasons not now known, Brettingham's two southern wings were never built. It has been suggested that the omission of these two wings was due to a last-minute economy. But that is unlikely, since Adam was commissioned to build an even larger stable-block nearby, as well as garden temples, a bridge over the lake, several lodges, a fishing-pavilion and the Home Farm. Nor can Adam have advised the change in plan. His south front was dependent upon the wings for the extra liveliness that they would have imparted to it, and the east and west elevations would also have gained greatly from them.

The north front, which one sees first when approaching the house from across the lake, is a grandiloquent Palladian façade of simple and (by that time) conventional design. A double exterior staircase rises to a portico formed by six columns mounted on a base of rusticated arches. This was Paine. On each side run the curved colonnades linking the main house to the family wing on the left and the kitchen wing on the right. This was Paine-cum-Brettingham. The only hint of Adam so far is his dome peeping over the top and five roundels which he added to the back wall of the portico above Paine's statue niches and front door. But on the other side of the house Adam entered into his own. He applied to this front his principle of 'movement', a combination of different shapes in three dimensions – columns with arches, domes with architraves, circular sweeping shapes with plain uprights and horizontals – breathing life throughout the building like a lung. It has been compared to a triumphal arch, both to its discredit and in its praise, but this is only one element. It is not Roman, but it borrows Roman ideas and transforms them. It is sturdy but decorative, firm but graceful. It is astonishing that something so heavy could contain something so light. It was quite revolutionary for its day, and Adam was barely thirty when he built it.

The interior of Kedleston is almost all Adam's work, and illustrates his monumental style to perfection. Having returned from his long visit to Italy only a couple of years before, his mind was full of Roman splendour, either in its original Augustan form or in Renaissance derivatives from it. His Marble Hall at Kedleston is an attempt to reproduce the effect of a Roman *atrium*, and his circular Saloon the *vestibulum*, in eighteenth-century terms. The twenty fluted monoliths of Nottinghamshire alabaster dominate the hall by their solemnity. It was not simply a place in which to leave your hat, but the still heart of a great house. In Elizabethan times such a hall would have been the centre of household life, but not at Kedleston: voices were not raised in this stupendous room, and functionally it had no purpose. 'Movement' was discarded, apart from the coved ceiling and three round skylights: even the fireplaces on each side were Adam's later additions. It is superbly empty, as if the very air which it encloses is an essential part of the design.

The Saloon, almost equally vast, makes quite a different effect, though it too is monumental in character. Here there is more decoration, less majesty. The coffered ceiling, rising sixty-two feet into the dome and lit by a spider's-web skylight at the apex, is the most satisfying geometrical design that can be seen anywhere in Adam's houses. The finish and spacing of the furniture, the lamp-brackets and Rebecca's chiaroscuro paintings, have been thought out with infinite care, and even the cast-iron stoves form pleasing silhouettes in the alcoves. They illustrate Robert Adam's inventiveness, his acute sense of what best fits a particular purpose, his capacity for quick variation between the grand and the domestic, between the elaborate and the merely pretty, and the obvious enjoyment with which he turned from one material to another – alabaster, marble, bronze, iron, wood, stucco, plaster, paint – contriving his exquisite designs from each in turn. They also illustrate the care with which the Curzon family have looked after this priceless possession during the five centuries of their occupation.

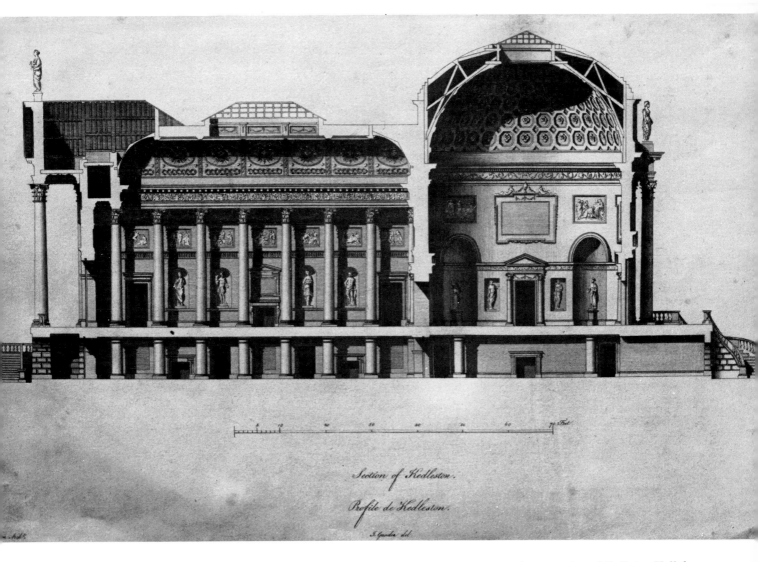

Section of Kedleston.

Profile de Kedleston.

J. Gandon del.

A cross-section of Kedleston Hall from
Vitruvius Britannicus, *showing the*
Marble Hall (left) and the domed
Saloon (right).

Mellerstain
Berwickshire

THAT ONE OF THE ADAM FAMILY should have built your home is a boast which every owner would be proud to make. But that two Adams should have collaborated on it at an interval of nearly fifty years is more than any man, even a Scottish nobleman, has the right to expect. Yet this in brief is the story of Mellerstain. William Adam began to build it for George Baillie in 1725. Robert Adam, his more famous son, finished it for Baillie's grandson (also George) in about 1770–5.

Of the two, Robert Adam has left on the house the deeper impress, not only because he built the larger part of it, but because he applied to its main rooms the infinite grace and care with which he touched everything that came under his hands. The interior, therefore, is the main attraction of Mellerstain – the interior and the garden. The exterior is in a sense a double disappointment. It is disappointing because the father was unable to complete the whole house as he designed it; and because Robert Adam chose for his additions the castellated style of which he never became so great a master as in his own version of the classical.

The contrast between William's work and Robert's is immediately seen on the northern, or entrance, front. The two wings which flank the forecourt are William Adam's; the main block which joins them is Robert's. The former are self-contained buildings, nearly square in shape, with cupolas rising over tiny internal courtyards. They are very simple, their rough walls as mealy as porridge and virtually unornamented, but instantly satisfying in their homeliness and proportions. The east wing was the family's house, the west the stables. The family wing is so modest that it contains not one room that can be identified as the main reception room, and the staircase is an apologetic stone spiral of which the turret juts out so awkwardly into the courtyard that it denies the latter any architectural distinction that it might have possessed. Even the horses in the other wing were more elegantly housed than this. But the simplicity, even humbleness, of these wings is explained by William Adam's drawings of the central block which was never executed. Here indeed was a noble pile, more in the Wren tradition than Vanbrugh's (with which William Adam was experimenting at the same time at Hopetoun). How easily the little wings would have lain alongside the main building!

The entrance front. The two wings—the family house on the left and a corner of the stables on the right—were built by William Adam in 1725 for George Baillie. The central block was added about 1775 by Robert Adam for Baillie's grandson.

One of the mysteries of Mellerstain is why William Adam's main house was never built. George Baillie the elder was rich, well connected, politically influential and married to a charming woman, Grisell Hume, who left upon contemporaries an impression of determination, efficiency and taste. She was a woman of high moral and physical courage, a poetess in her own right, and a formidable housekeeper. Yet she ruled over nothing more than one small wing. Between it and the stable-block was a void, 'the intended house', as Richard Pococke described it after a visit to Mellerstain in 1760. The problem deepens when we learn that during the whole of the interval between the beginning and the finishing of the house a majestic park was being laid out around it with a vista southwards over a great lake cupped in beautifully wooded hills. Its appearance can be guessed from a plan of the grounds made four years before Pococke's visit. To the north is a starred and tonsured wood; to the south the rectangle of the lake. In the centre is the terminating circle of the approach drive. Minuscule below its bottom arc, are two hatchured blocks: these are the wings. Between them extends 'the intended house', a gravelled continuation of the drive, a mere emptiness.

Whatever the reason for his grandparents' strange system of priorities, George Baillie determined to fill the gap soon after he succeeded to the estate in 1759. He called in Robert Adam. So Adam the younger designed for Baillie the younger a large house which incorporated his father's wings but bridged them by a domesticated castle instead of by the classical building which his father had intended. The building is stern, even tough; an anachronistic throwback to Border peel-towers. It is not in any sense Gothic, in which the Adam brothers showed little interest even when it became the fashion of the times; it is not even romantic, like Adam's Culzean Castle in Ayrshire; it is more Georgianized Tudor, faintly reminiscent of the exterior of Syon, where Robert Adam had been working ten years before. The walls are so roughly finished, with quoins and window-labels of odd sizes set at careless angles and without a single swag or medallion to gratify what we have now come to expect of him, that one suspects that they may have been intended as a base for a stucco finish. Some doubt could exist whether it was really Adam's work, did not his original designs survive in the Soane Museum to prove it.

The second mystery of Mellerstain is why it is so thin. It is one room, and one corridor, wide, with bulkier angle-towers and a thickened centre for the hall and staircase. There was space on its platform for a house of more normal proportions, and one can only guess that the Baillies desired a house that would look bigger from outside than it actually was, and would remain manageable without too large a staff. The result is that the main reception rooms extend in a long line all along the south side, leading one into the other, with a connecting corridor running the full length of the house behind them. The pattern is repeated on the bedroom floor above. On the top storey of the central tower is the largest and one of the loveliest rooms in the whole house, a long gallery as splendid as a ballroom, with superb views over the garden.

Each of the main living-rooms was decorated by Robert Adam with a delicacy that holds the visitor in thrall to his superlative talent. The rooms do

The small drawing-room, once of the suite of rooms by Robert Adam which runs the length of the south front.

The central design of the ceiling in the music room.

not depend upon his usual contrast between straight lines and curved, coved ceilings and flat. The only departures from the rectangular shapes are the apses of the entrance hall, and the Ionic screens and coved ceiling of the long gallery. The other rooms are basically boxes of different sizes. In none of his houses is Adam's sense of colour more brilliantly displayed. The rooms are made by the decoration of walls, ceilings and fireplaces, but the reliefs of plaster and marble are so shallow that they would be almost insignificant but for their contrasted colouring. There is one room, Lady Haddington's private sitting-room, where the decoration is unpainted (perhaps deliberately, but more likely left unfinished or overpainted in white at a later period) and the most exquisite shells, harps, garlands and other devices seem as bleak as moulds without their gilding or background painting. But in the library, undoubtedly the finest room in the house and among Adam's very greatest creations, the reliefs spring to life. One would know it immediately for an

A general view of the Library, one of the most beautiful eighteenth-century rooms in Europe. Over the left-hand door is a bust by Roubiliac of Lady Grisell Baillie, wife of the first owner of Mellerstain. It was carved in 1746 when she was aged 81.

Adam room and yet one finds in it decorative inventions that have no parallel in his work elsewhere, particularly the broad friezes above the book-cases containing long panels of Homeric scenes and busts set in recessed circles framed by squares. This wonderful room also illustrates how well Adam's decorations combine with present-day furniture. Such rooms need the addition of solids like sofas or the larger type of writing-desk, for without them the decoration can sometimes appear over-sweet.

Mellerstain, in short, is a jewel set in a block of rough-hewn stone, and is laid on a carpet of incomparable texture and variety. The contrast between the garden, the house and the rooms will strike every visitor. The first and the third are the products of the subtlest design: the house is by contrast of little more than academic interest. But the combination of the three is a memorial to two generations of two families who worked together to create something of enduring value.

Althorp
Northamptonshire

FIFTEEN GENERATIONS OF SPENCERS have inhabited this house. Allowing for brothers succeeding brothers, and the same men holding in succession two different titles, there have been at Althorp, since the early sixteenth century, five Knights, three Barons Spencer, five Earls of Sunderland, seven Earls Spencer and one Duke of Marlborough, and the descent has never wavered from the direct male line. Many of them have been distinguished in public life. The second Earl of Sunderland was Charles II's and William III's leading Minister; his son, the third Earl, who married the great Marlborough's daughter, was Secretary-of-State to Queen Anne and George I; the third Earl Spencer led the House of Commons during the Reform Bill debates of 1830–4; and the fifth Earl Spencer, having held a number of high offices in the later part of the reign of Queen Victoria, was leader of the Liberal Peers from 1902 to 1905. Almost every one of them, to a greater or lesser degree, has been an enlightened patron of the arts, and two, the third Earl of Sunderland and the second Earl Spencer, assembled libraries which were among the most famous of their times.

The house reflects the Spencers' artistic interests and their marriages with other great English families more than their political activities. There could scarcely be room for both. The furniture, sculpture, books, porcelain and, above all, the pictures fill the walls, and many of the rooms were designed or remodelled to show them off to best advantage. This description is not directly concerned with the works of art, though they will be evident in the photographs. They are the chief glory of Althorp, forming one of the greatest family collections in the world.

Althorp, like the family's history and art-collection, is the product of the slow assimilation of changing fortunes and tastes. It has been the same house for more than four centuries, in the sense that the site is the same and the basic structure is Elizabethan. Parts of an even earlier but smaller house, built of the local orange stone, is hidden in its core, the house which the first Sir John Spencer bought in 1508 and which dated back unfathomable centuries. It was surrounded by a moat, which survived until 1790. Early in the reign of Queen Elizabeth I, his grandson, another Sir John, greatly enlarged the manor-house which he inherited, adding the two wings which still enclose its forecourt, a

The entrance front. The original mediaeval manor-house was reconstructed in 1573 when the two projecting wings were added. In about 1790 the whole house was re-faced by Henry Holland and two corridors were added on the side of the forecourt and the pediment over the entrance.

long gallery (now the Picture Gallery) and other rooms around an open central court, on the far side of his Great Hall. The whole was built in red brick with stone dressings, concealing the mediaeval stone and timbering behind its central part. When the present hall was recently repaired, roof-timbers, possibly dating from the fourteenth century, were found above it. Although it is possible by a process of mental X-ray to discern the Elizabethan buildings behind the present façades, nobody could guess without investigation that this is one of the most continuously occupied sites in Northamptonshire, or indeed in the whole country. It looks like a splendid product of the two grand centuries of English architecture and landscaping, the seventeenth and eighteenth, and such, in effect, it is. The changes that were made to the house externally have stamped it with an Augustan character, although its origins were a great deal earlier.

The Vorstermans painting of 1677 well illustrates the transition between the old and the present appearance of Althorp. The moat still ran round all four sides of its platform, and the main walls were still of sixteenth-century brick. But when the picture was painted, the Elizabethan house had recently been transformed by the second Earl of Sunderland into a palace 'disposed after the Italian manner'. The gable-ended wings had been altered into typically Restoration hipped roofs with a balustrade, the upper windows were topped by arched pediments, and classical pilasters clung to the wall between them. To the east, formal walled gardens stretched outwards towards the park, in the design of which André le Nôtre is said to have had a hand. Internally the Earl modernized the house by improving the staircase within the central courtyard and laid out the state-rooms on the first floor of the north side, comprising the Saloon or Great Room, two large bedrooms at each end, a waiting-room and a dressing-room.

It was one of the few houses to meet with the approval of Duke Cosimo of Tuscany's courtiers in 1669. It 'may be said to be the best planned and best arranged country seat in the kingdom', they reported. 'For although there may be many which surpass it in size, none are superior to it in symmetrical elegance.' John Evelyn was equally enthusiastic:

The house or rather palace at Althorp is a noble uniform pile in form of a half H, built of brick and freestone balustered and *à la moderne*; the hall is well, the staircase excellent; the rooms of state, galleries, offices and furniture such as may become a great prince. It is situate in the midst of a garden exquisitely planted and kept, and all this in a park walled in with hewn stone, planted with rows or walks of trees, canals, and fishponds and stored with game.

When Celia Fiennes visited the house in 1702, the year of the second Earl's death, she described it as 'like a Prince's Court of brick and stone very fine, with a large Parke wall'd in of a good extent'. Already it was filled with many of the most valuable pieces of its art-collection, for the second Earl, during his travels in Italy and Holland, and as Ambassador in Paris and Madrid, had many opportunities to indulge his tastes as a collector.

The next stage came in the early eighteenth century, when the fifth Earl of Sunderland, later third Duke of Marlborough, altered the entrance hall,

Althorp in 1677 by John Vorstermans. It shows the appearance of the house soon after its reconstruction in the Restoration period. The Elizabethan brickwork and pre-Tudor moat were then still visible.

possibly with the advice of Colen Campbell, and commissioned John Wootton to paint the huge hunting pictures, which, like those at Longleat, show the continuous interest taken by the family in field-sports. He also built the splendid stable-block of local stone with two classical porticoes at its north and east sides, and the charming gardener's cottage with its three-arched porch. But the Elizabethan-Restoration façades stayed until nearly the end of the eighteenth century. Their mellowed red brick glowed richly across the park.

When George John Spencer succeeded as the second Earl Spencer in 1783, part of the house had exhibited alarming signs of disintegration, and repair work was urgently required. He called in Henry Holland to advise him. 'At first', wrote the Earl, 'we thought we must be content with making the apartments we live in weather-proof and saving the house from tumbling down. We have got Mr Holland here who has brought his plans with him. I have a notion that they will be very clever ones . . . but the Quomodo is the difficulty.' Holland was a young man of talents, exceptional good looks, grace of bearing, charm of manner and unusual powers of persuasion. He was not content merely to prop up a beautiful house, but induced his patron to alter it inside and out, at an eventual Quomodo of £20,257, by a transformation as radical as any since the additions of the second Earl of Sunderland over a hundred years before.

Holland's main external change was to cover up the Elizabethan brick with silvery-white facing tiles, known technically as 'rebate-tiles' but popularly as 'mathematical-tiles', with which he refaced Sloane Place, his own house in London. His motives were two: as a protection against the weather, which they assuredly were; and because a prejudice, originated by Isaac Ware in 1756, had condemned plain brick as a surfacing for country-houses of the noblest kind. 'The colour,' wrote Ware, 'is fiery . . . and in summer has an appearance of heat that is very disagreeable.' Moreover, 'there is something harsh in the transition from red brick to stone, and it seems altogether unnatural.' Compton Wynyates, Blickling, Weston! So Althorp, to its present disadvantage, was refaced by brick-tiles. Behind them are the original Elizabethan bricks, and behind them again are the stone and half-timber of the pre-Tudor house. Althorp was assuming its present appearance. Holland added pediments to the centre of the entrance and garden fronts, and tall pilasters to the former. He filled in the moat, widened the windows and built corridors along the inner sides of both wings, which narrow the forecourt but add greatly to the charm and convenience of the interior. Furthermore, in 1790 he completely remodelled the reception rooms on the ground floor of the west wing by throwing the Long Library into the Yellow Drawing-room and South Drawing-room. Later, exceptionally wide doors were added which can be left open to form a long gallery of great variety and friendliness. These three rooms are the most pleasant in the whole house and contain many of its finest possessions. When the ceilings were refashioned in 1864 by Broadbent of Leicester, Victorian standards scarcely dropped below those of Holland himself.

Althorp is a house of the greatest interest in its history, ownership, architecture and contents. Its setting between formal gardens and in the middle of a park that is the quintessence of all that is loveliest in the Midland countryside, make it a house that deserves contemplation, just as if it were a picture on one of its own walls. It has a ready-made dignity which immediately proclaims it to be the house of a great family, but its charm is much more subtle. Even Holland's brick-tiling must originally have glowed in the sun before it became discoloured. The rooms are large, numerous and some of them grand, but one can still agree with Cosimo's companions that it is the 'best-planned and best-arranged seat in the kingdom'. At every doorway one experiences a sense of surprise, of delight, but never of shock. It is a good-mannered house, and its present owner, Earl Spencer, has cherished it and loved it as all his many ancestors did before him.

*The Yellow Drawing-room, looking through to the
South Drawing-room*

Plas Newydd
Isle of Anglesey

THE FIRST SURPRISE OF PLAS NEWYDD, and a visitor's most lasting recollection of it, is its site. It lies on a slope above the Menai Strait, and the approach to it on foot is downhill to the front door. Suddenly, as the trees part and the gradient steepens, a view of water and mountains is revealed which has few equals in Britain. The distant skyline is the crest of Snowdonia. The foreground is the strait. Snowdon itself, humped at the shoulders, terminates a serpent-back of neighbouring hills, which are sometimes cloud-capped, sometimes snow-capped, sometimes rounded and brown. The strait is more like a wide river than an arm of the sea, and upon it there is normally a sailing-boat or some craft making its way from Liverpool or Caernarvon. The opposite shore, which forms part of the Vaynol estate, is open to fields which slope to the water's edge with great woods behind. Two bridges, of which one, Robert Stephenson's railway bridge of 1850, is visible from the house a mile away, link Anglesey to the mainland like hyphens. When one wakes in the house, the first glance from its windows is always a renewed delight, since the more familiar the view, the more sensitive is one's reaction to subtle changes of season, climate and light.

Plas Newydd, owing to its position, origins and associations, is a distinguished house. The front which faces the water and mountains, with its swelling apses, turrets and well-ruled bay-windows, is undeniably handsome. Therefore one regrets the changes which have transfigured the entrance front into something more puzzling and plain. The lovely pale-grey stable, built by Joseph Potter in 1797 and left unaltered, is a reminder of what we have lost by the later decision to enlarge the house and de-Gothicize it. The original shape is still there, but it needs some disentangling.

There was a house here in the sixteenth century, of which the double cellars survive and perhaps some of the interior walls. Towers and semicircular bays were added at intervals in its long history, and in 1793–9 James Wyatt ingeniously pulled them together to create a lovely symmetrical house romanticized by crenellations, pinnacled turrets and two symmetrical entrance porches each side of the sixteenth-century hall. At the same time he extensively remodelled the interior. A few years later his collaborator Joseph Potter added a chapel at the north end, and Humphrey Repton was consulted on the layout of the garden and the park.

The house stands on a sloping bank above the Menai Strait, facing the distant range of Snowdonia.

This was the house that stood externally unchanged throughout the nineteenth century. In the 1930s the sixth Marquess of Anglesey, influenced perhaps by the fashionable distaste for late-eighteenth-century Gothic, replaced the battlements by a plain parapet, shortened the pinnacles and gave them Tudor caps, and heightened the north wing in a blunt style which altered and (it must be admitted) marred the appearance of the house from the entrance side, though greatly adding to its convenience and comfort within. He also built a screen-wall at right angles to this façade which split the forecourt in two. The result was to confuse the eye and rob the house of much of its former grace, a grace which it undoubtedly needs, for the approach to it is from above, starting at roof-level, an awkward direction from which to see any house for the first time. Repton was right to comment that such an approach needs an irregularity of outline which Potter and Wyatt gave to the enchanting stables. To his ever-lasting credit, however, the sixth Marquess commissioned Rex Whistler to decorate the walls of the dining-room with a masterpiece of contemporary art.

Inside the front door Wyatt's and Potter's remodelling makes a first impression of experiment and serenity. The Gothic hall, high and ribbed, with a latticed gallery at one end at first-floor level, well marks the transition from outside to inside. It is theatrical and relatively empty of furniture, a mental preparation for the more habitable rooms beyond. Opening directly from it is the Music Room, an even larger hall created from the sixteenth-century hall, but broadened by several feet, fan-vaulted, with tall windows along one side and furnished with large paintings including two portraits, one by Lawrence and the other by Hoppner, of the first Marquess of Anglesey, the commander of Wellington's cavalry at Waterloo, where in the last moments of the battle he lost a leg.

These are the two main Gothic rooms. The rest of the house is treated more conventionally. It is difficult and unnecessary to attach to individual rooms any central date, for they have been adapted and redecorated at different periods to form on the ground floor a suite which alternates between rooms for common use and rooms for privacy – a large bow-windowed drawing-room, a library, and a lovely red room which Lady Anglesey used until recently as her sitting-room. On the first floor, the bedrooms extend along both sides of the house, each with its attendant bathroom (Plas Newydd is said to be the only house in Britain which contains more bathrooms than bedrooms), but most face the Menai Strait, the apsed windows and bays opening on the splendid views with which this account began. Two of them are shown to the public, the former bedrooms of the Marquess and Marchioness. Lord Anglesey's contains a superb bed of the late seventeenth century, brought from Beaudesert in Staffordshire, the family's other house which was demolished in 1935. Lady Anglesey's bedroom, which was redecorated in the 1930s with the advice of Sibyl Colefax, owes its delicacy to muslin bed-hangings, sheepskin rugs and huge pale-pink cushions tossed on to white armchairs. The plasterwood frieze of loose acanthus scrolls and the chimneypiece survive from the Wyatt-Potter decorations of the 1790s.

The Octagon Room in the south-east tower. Until recently it was used by Lady Anglesey as her study.

The upper storey of the house was transformed into a self-contained flat when Lord Anglesey gave Plas Newydd to the National Trust in 1976. It represents a model solution to the problem of a great house now too large to inhabit totally. The family have safeguarded their privacy in fewer and smaller rooms, which have the best views because they lie highest; and the public is allowed the freedom of the grander part of the house which is all the lovelier now that doors can be left open room to room, and the length and lightness of the ground floor is revealed. From part of the previous servants' quarters Lord Anglesey, the historian of the British cavalry, has constructed a fine museum of military accoutrements, including the wooden articulated leg that substituted for the flesh and bone which his famous ancestor left on the field of Waterloo, and the trousers which he wore on that memorable day, still caked with the battlefield's mud.

The Rex Whistler dining-room lies towards one end of the house, opening on the garden-front. It is a long and fairly narrow room, lit by five windows which illuminate Whistler's huge oil-painting on the opposite wall, and two short side-walls which continue the theme of the main painting by *trompe-l'oeil* arcades. Rex Whistler began this stupendous work, the major legacy of his very individual art, in 1937, and finished it shortly before the outbreak of the war in which he was killed. He painted the main canvas, fifty-eight feet long, in London, mounting it on rollers in the studio of a theatrical scenery-painter, and added directly to the room's surfaces the ornamental panels of the side-walls and simulated coffering of the ceiling.

The scene is a land and sea-scape, Mediterranean in inspiration, but echoing the view of Snowdonia which it faces. A harbour and a city dominate the foreground, islands and ships the middle-distance, and a mountainous

The Rex Whistler room which was
converted in 1935 from servants' rooms
into a long dining-room. In 1937 Rex
Whistler painted for the wall opposite the
windows a mural fifty-eight feet long,
and decorated the rest of the room in a
corresponding style.

landscape spotted with castellated villages lies beyond. It is a romance, but
Whistler executed it with the utmost care, contriving without fault the difficult
perspectives of so long a scene, and the details of the buildings and shipping
with which he filled his city and its harbour. It is dateless. There are steam-
ships and a gondola, but no cars; Renaissance palaces, but no overtly
twentieth-century accretions. The painting is an architectural jumble, but it
does not strain credulity. It is neat but informal: a town at work. Here and
there in his painting are found bundles of merchandise, and weeds growing in
cracks between the nearer paving stones. One can take imaginary walks
through the town, recognizing at intervals famous monuments like Trajan's
column, the steeple of St Martin's-in-the-Fields, the Round Tower of Windsor
Castle, and sometimes fantasies based on Whistler's recollection of houses
and public buildings which, once seen, were imprinted with almost photographic precision on his memory. There are jokes too, like a boy stealing an
apple from a fruiterer's shop, a cigarette still burning on a step as if he had just
left it there, and the prints of wet bare feet, where Neptune has apparently
walked off the canvas into the room. There are compliments to the family, in
the equestrian statue of Lord Anglesey standing in the main square, recording
his 'foundation of the city', and less grandly, the family's dogs and the
Marchioness's spectacles lying beside her book. Rex Whistler himself appears
in one corner as a gardener leaning on a broom-handle.

Part of the elaborate townscape which Rex Whistler painted for the long wall of the dining-room. The equestrian statue on the left is Whistler's tribute to his patron, the sixth Marquess of Anglesey.

Plas Newydd is no longer the 'new place' that its Welsh name signifies. It has an ancient history of building and rebuilding, of constant redecoration, and of continuous occupation by a family who have seldom remained satisfied with what they knew in their childhood. They took architectural risks, and sometimes made mistakes; they made imaginative use of the decorative fashions of their times; and in the present generation they have discovered a happy compromise between privacy and display. It is not the most beautiful house described in this book, but its setting can compare only with St Michael's Mount for drama and unspoiled grandeur, and under the care of the National Trust its many rooms, great and small, have been brought to a new perfection which everyone can now enjoy.

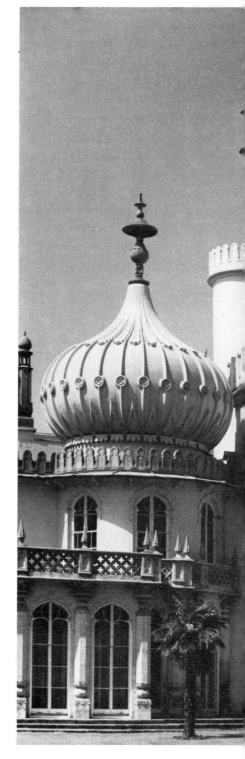

The Royal
Pavilion
Brighton, Sussex

THE PAVILION HAS BECOME an accepted part of the Brighton scene. It goes with the elegant, indolent, faintly raffish atmosphere of the sunlit promenades. The last few hundred yards of the London road, before it is extended out to sea by the leaping extravagances of the pier, are enlivened by a gleaming pile of domes and minarets rising from a lawn. The dullest mind would wonder what it could be. An amusement arcade, a temporary exhibition ground, a fair, a folly? It is none of these things. It is a former royal palace. It is by far the greatest, almost the only, example of a style that flashed across English architectural history at the beginning of the nineteenth century to die out like a rocket in a trail of sparks. It contains decorations and furniture which for all their fantasy form the most brilliant expression of the revolt against classicism. It is romantic and exotic, Coleridge's pleasure-dome translated from Xanadu to an English seaside resort. Most remarkable of all – since such a building, one might suppose, could only have been erected by someone with more money to spend than position to sustain – it was built for the heir to the British throne and Empire by John Nash, the creator of the classic terraces around Regent's Park.

The Royal Pavilion had its origins in an illness and a romance. The Prince of Wales, later Prince Regent and still later George IV, first came to Brighton for his health in 1783, when he was persuaded that sea-water was a cure for glandular swellings of the neck. Two years later he secretly married Mrs Fitzherbert, the twenty-five-year-old daughter of a Roman Catholic family, who had already been twice widowed, and brought her to Brighton in a hopeless attempt to economize (his debts already amounted to over half-a-million pounds) and to enjoy his unavowed marriage in comparative privacy. He rented a small farmhouse in the Steine, a broad strip of lawn that ran down to the sea. In 1787, such was his ungovernable love of society, he decided to rebuild the house in a style fit to receive his friends. As his architect he employed Henry Holland, who between April and July in that year ran up a bow-fronted house in the classical manner, topped by a shallow dome. It was already known as the Prince's 'marine pavilion', as if to stress its primarily flippant intent. This house became the core of the vastly larger and more elaborate palace that was to be built around it. You can still see behind its

The east façade which, unlike the other fronts, is perfectly symmetrical. John Nash made brilliant use of fretted stonework which casts dappled shadows on the wall behind.

oriental encrustations the shape of Holland's pretty Palladian villa. Its loveliest room, the oval Saloon, has survived structurally intact, though unrecognizable in its decoration. Somewhere embedded in the walls must be part of the original farm-house. Never can a yeoman's dwelling have undergone such a metamorphosis.

In the course of the next thirty-five years, Holland's building was transformed, slowly at the start and then with gathering speed. The first change was the addition of two further oval rooms at either end, and of green-painted iron canopies to the balconies, the originals of that charming Regency vogue that spread rapidly through Brighton and then to the entire country. In 1802 the Prince was given a roll of Chinese wallpaper, and he made for it a Chinese gallery in the northern wing. This was the beginning of the oriental decorations. Gradually Chinese motifs spread throughout the house. Chinese furniture was brought down from Carlton House, where the Prince had already begun experimenting with the style; Chinese mantelpieces and bamboo panelling were installed; works of art were imported from China itself, including more wallpaper, porcelain and huge pieces of highly coloured statuary. By 1803 the entire interior had been redecorated in this manner. The press and public scoffed, but the house was acknowledged by the ebullient circle of the Prince's friends to be an outstanding success. So entranced was he by its bazaar-like interior, that he toyed with the idea of encasing the whole house in a Chinese pagoda. William Porden was commissioned to do it.

Before Porden's plans had advanced beyond the stage of sketches, the Prince's Chinese tastes succumbed to his discovery of the Indian. He first allowed Porden to build an immense stable and riding-school in the Indian, or more properly, Moorish, manner, and then complained that his horses were better housed than he was himself. So first Humphrey Repton, and then John Nash, were invited to design a new exterior for the Pavilion which was to stand comparison not only with the stables but with the greatest monuments of Delhi itself. Repton's designs, to his great mortification, were not used, but they contained the germ of Nash's later and more subtle interpretation. In the final version, there was to be a great onion-dome over the Saloon with two smaller ones on each side, flanked by two other domes over a new banqueting-room to the south and music-room to the north. The building was started in 1825 and was almost finished five years later, the year in which the Prince Regent succeeded to the throne. The total cost had by that time amounted to over half a million pounds.

The Indian exterior does not clash with the Chinese interior because both were western conceptions of the Orient as a whole. The Pavilion could have been built in a Russian, Japanese, Persian or even Egyptian style without making much difference to the total effect. There was no literal imitation of anything. The very shape of the onion-domes was a deliberate refinement of the Indian originals illustrated in Thomas and William Daniell's *Views of Oriental Scenery* which made so great an impact on contemporary taste. Those on the extreme north and south of the building had no prototype whatever east of Suez. As few visitors to Brighton were likely to go to India or China, there

The Banqueting Room. The most ambitious and elaborate of the Chinoiserie decorations executed by Nash. The wall paintings and the chandelier, which weighs over a ton, are by Robert Jones.

was little risk of pedantic comparisons, and the gaps in the architect's knowledge could be filled, to the building's great advantage, by his own fancy. Cobbett thought the Pavilion a copy of the Kremlin. William Daniell himself, one of the few critics competent to judge, exclaimed indignantly that 'there is not a feature great or small which at all accords with the purity, grandeur and magnificence that characterize the genuine Oriental style'. Hazlitt described it as a collection of stone pumpkins and pepperboxes; while to Sidney Smith has been attributed the most famous comment of all, 'The dome of St Paul's must have come down to Brighton and pupped.' Since then ridicule of the Pavilion has become as unfashionable as its style.

There is a marked difference in the two decorative phases of the interior. When the Prince's exuberance was at its height, he favoured a barbaric splendour that recalls the colour-plates of a child's edition of Marco Polo. The two largest rooms, the banqueting and music rooms, look as if they had been put up at a circus for the Christmas season, until one discovers the excellence of the materials and workmanship and the refinement of much of the detail. But those who find themselves appalled by such grotesque display will soon be reconciled to the Pavilion by the exquisite *chinoiserie* of the smaller rooms in the centre and upstairs. One does not need to have a taste for the Orient to appreciate these rooms; only an eye for decorative pattern and colour, and the imagination to recapture the excitement with which these new designs were conceived and executed. What fun they had! What shapes a dragon's tail could be made to assume, since nobody had ever seen one! What variations one could play on Regency Gothic, since the point of the building was that all existing rules should be broken!

Yet there remained a basic discipline. The east façade, one discovers with some surprise, is perfectly symmetrical. The fireplaces, though the chimneys be shaped like minarets, must not smoke. The kitchen, though decorated with cast-iron palm-trees, must serve banquets punctually and hot. If one of the huge chandeliers were allowed to fall, it might kill a king. Perhaps during the building of the Pavilion tempers became frayed, as during rehearsals of a harlequinade. It was a serious attempt at fun, and therefore full of pitfalls.

Now that the Pavilion is open to the public and much of its original furniture and decoration restored, it is seen to be the most magical house in Britain. The habitual glumness of custodians of public buildings is absent here; it is as if something of the Prince Regent's unashamed extravagance and delight in people and things has entered their souls and kept them perpetually amused.

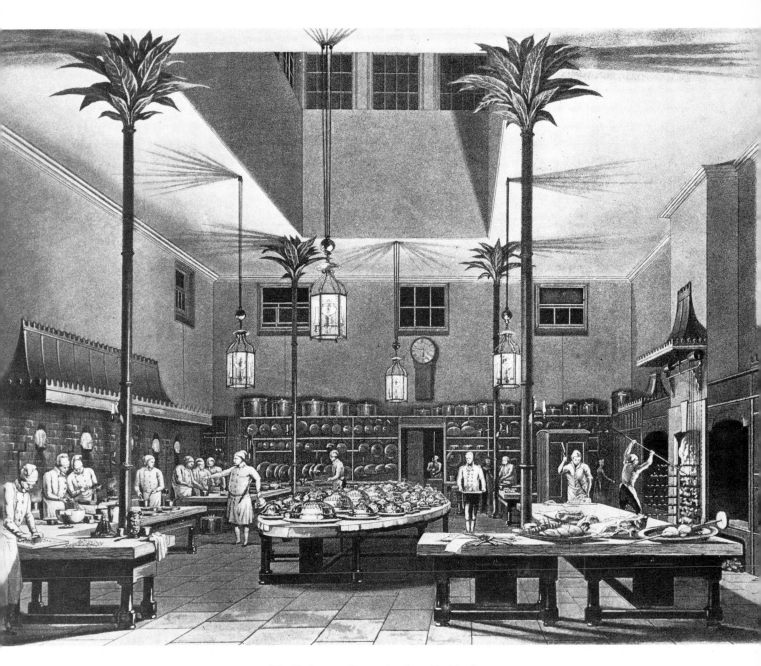

The kitchen, an illustration from Nash's views of the Royal Pavilion. The roof is supported by four iron columns representing palm trees, with leaves of sheet bronze. Many of the original fittings in the kitchen have survived to this day.

Acknowledgements

The author and publishers are greatly indebted to the owners or tenants of the houses for permission to include them in this book. The National Trust owns sixteen of these houses (as shown in the contents list).
For the other houses thanks is given to the following:

Ightham Mote Mr C. H. Robinson
Haddon Hall The Duke of Rutland
Penshurst Place Viscount De L'Isle vc
Compton Wynyates The Marquess of Northampton
Longleat The Marquess of Bath
Sulgrave Manor The Sulgrave Manor Board
Castle Fraser The National Trust for Scotland (Major and Mrs Michael Smiley)
Hatfield House The Marquess of Salisbury
Wilton House The Earl of Pembroke
Weston Park The Earl of Bradford
Belton House Lord Brownlow
Chatsworth The Duke of Devonshire
Castle Howard Mr George Howard
Easton Neston Lord Hesketh
Blenheim Palace The Duke of Marlborough
Ditchley Park The Ditchley Foundation
Holkham Hall The Earl of Leicester
Syon House The Duke of Northumberland
Kedleston Hall The Viscount Scarsdale
Mellerstain The Earl of Haddington
Althorp The Earl Spencer
The Royal Pavilion The County Borough of Brighton

Photographs were supplied and are reproduced by kind permission of the following (numbers refer to pages – italics to pages with colour photographs):

Aerofilms 9, 72, 94; Peter Baker Photography 55 *bottom*; Lionel Bell 271, 273, 275; John Bethell *54, 182–3, 184, 191 top, 238, 281*; Brighton Corporation 287; British Tourist Authority 29, 168 *top*; Courtauld Institute 160; Kerry Dundas 10, 12, 13, 20, 22 *top and bottom*, 23, *36*, 38, 44, 46, 47 *left and right*, 51, 52, *53, 55 top, 56*, 57, 60, 74, 77, 100, 102, 104, *109*, 118–9, 140–1, 138, 141, 148, 150, 151, 153, 158, 166, 174, 176, 178, 195, 197, 199, 200, 201, 204 *top and bottom*, 208, 209, 211, 213, 215, *219*, 221, 227, 230, 242, 243, 244, 256, 260, 261, 263, 265, 283; Geoff Goode Photographics 117, 132 *top*, 134, *163*, 232, 233, 235, 236, *237*; Ian Graham *210*; Angelo Hornak *218*; A. F. Kersting 33, *34, 35*, 62, 107, *161, 162*, 167, 168 *bottom*, 225, 299, *240*, 267, 268, 269, 285; Manchester Airviews 186; National Trust 15 (Olive Kitson), 16 (Olive Kitson), 17 (Olive Kitson), 40 (Jeremy Whitaker), 42 (Aerofilms), 58 (Country Life), 65 (Edwin Smith), 76 *top and bottom*, *89, 90, 92*, 98, *110, 111*, 120 *top and bottom*, 132 *bottom*, 135 (Jeremy Whitaker), 136 (Jeremy Whitaker), 143, 144, 145, 146 (Algernon Smith), 155, 157, *164, 181*, 191 *bottom* (Edwin Smith), 172 (Country Life), 179 *top* (Jeremy Whitaker), 179 *bottom* (Country Life), 205 (A. F. Kersting), 207 (John Bethell), 220 (by courtesy of IPC), 222 (Edwin Smith), 223 (Edwin Smith), *239*, 247 (Jeremy Whitaker), 248 (Courtauld Institute), 249, 251, 252 (John Bethell), 277, 279 (John Bethell), 280 (John Bethell), 281 (John Bethell); National Trust for Scotland 80, 82, 83, 85, *91*; Photo Precision 97; By kind permission of the Marquess of Salisbury 108, *112*; Edwin Smith 87, 88, 95, 124 *bottom*, 126, 189, 192, 193, 254, 257; Sulgrave Manor Board 67, 68, 69; Jeremy Whitaker 26, 28, 31, 41, 63; Derrick Witty 113, 114, 123, 128, 130; By courtesy of Worcester College, Oxford 124 top